ART OF
WINNING

Dr Radhakrishnan Pillai is a certified management consultant from the International Institute of Management Consultants and Director, Chanakya International Institute of Leadership Studies (CIILS) at the University of Mumbai. He is an expert in Chanakya studies and is the author of the bestselling Chanakya series which includes *Chanakya in Daily Life, Corporate Chanakya, Chanakya in the Classroom, Chanakya's 7 Secrets of Leadership, Chanakya in You, Katha Chanakya, Inside Chanakya's Mind: Aanvikshiki and the Art of Thinking, Thus Spoke Chanakya* and *Chatur Chanakya & the Himalayan Problem*. He lives in Mumbai.

He tweets at the handle @rchanakyapillai and is also active on all other social media platforms.

ART OF WINNING

The Chanakya Way

RADHAKRISHNAN PILLAI

RUPA

Published by
Rupa Publications India Pvt. Ltd 2021
7/16, Ansari Road, Daryaganj
New Delhi 110002

Sales centres:
Allahabad Bengaluru Chennai
Hyderabad Jaipur Kathmandu
Kolkata Mumbai

ISBN: 978-93-91256-47-0

Third impression 2022

10 9 8 7 6 5 4 3

The moral right of the author has been asserted.

Printed in India

*Dedicated to the
hidden winner inside you*

CONTENTS

INTRODUCTION:
HOW IMPORTANT IS WINNING?

Chanakya—What is the first impression you get when you think of him?

I have asked this question in every leadership and management training programme that I have conducted. There are various answers that I get: an economist, strategist, kingmaker, teacher, politician, statesman, creator of the golden era of India where it was called *sone ki chidiya* (golden bird), the author of *Arthashastra* and the one who dethroned King Dhana Nanda of the Nanda dynasty that ruled the Magadha Empire and crowned his student Chandragupta Maurya.

The answers about their first impressions could be summed up in one word or one line. Some people would also go on to tell a story about him in detail. And my general response to such discussions would be, 'All of you are right. He has various dimensions to his personality and it is worth exploring him from different angles. He was all of the qualities put together.'

I would then start my session with a presentation on the life of Chanakya, mostly covering the following general points:

- Born in the fourth century BC in India
- Known by three names: Vishnugupta, Kautilya and Chanakya

- Defeated Alexander and Dhana Nanda of Magadha (modern-day Bihar)
- Kingmaker of Chandragupta Maurya
- Authored *Arthashastra* and *Chanakya Neeti*

After this I would generally conclude by saying, 'I am not a historian and would not have much to contribute about his life story. But my research on Chanakya is about the books that he authored: *Arthashastra* and *Chanakya Neeti*. I have been fortunate enough to study all 6,000 sutras (formulas) written in *Arthashastra*.'

Most of the eyebrows in the room would go up when I would say that I have studied all 6,000 sutras, and that too in chaste Sanskrit. I had studied *Arthashastra* under the personal guidance of Dr Gangadharan Nair (the dean of Sree Sankaracharya University of Sanskrit, Kerala) from the Chinmaya International Foundation, Kerala, and later proceeded to do my master's in Sanskrit and a PhD in *Arthashastra* under the guidance of Dr Shubhada Joshi (Head, Department of Philosophy, University of Mumbai, Maharashtra).

I would continue saying, 'I was fortunate that I have been learning and teaching *Arthashastra* for over 20 years now. And today, I even head the Chanakya International Institute of Leadership Studies (CIILS) at the University of Mumbai, where *Arthashastra* is taught as a formal subject of leadership. I have been also fortunate to start this institute in the University of Mumbai.'

By this time, the audience would generally take me and my study about Chanakya's teachings seriously. And then, after creating my first typical scholarly impression with my academic achievements, I would turn back and say, 'Let us keep all this aside for the time being. Do you know what my impression of Chanakya is after trying to understand him as a life-long commitment?'

The audience would generally wait for my answer with curiosity.

And I would say, 'If you truly understand Chanakya, you will never understand what failure is. He teaches you to be a winner again and again and again.'

It can often be seen as an over-exaggeration. How can a person be a winner all the time? We have heard that life is all about ups and downs, about success and failures. Winning and losing are the two sides of the same coin. Yes, this is true from one standpoint, there is no denying that. However, with Chanakya's wisdom, winning can become a habit rather than an exceptional outcome. I have seen this reflected in my own life. Unbelievable, but true.

I have worked on over 300 projects around Chanakya and his teachings. Be it writing 15 books, making movies, academic projects, business applications of Chanakya's theories and what not, *all* projects have been successful. I have also seen that if you plan well ahead and adopt the right strategy, it will surely be a success. Moreover, having multiple backup plans helps us to be a winner all the way.

Is this possible for you as well? Yes, of course. The winning formulas of Chanakya have existed for nearly 2,400 years and they are still relevant in our era. To understand Chanakya, the only requirement is a 'strategic mindset'. Please note that I am not saying that you require a 'positive mindset'. Of course, being positive is a very important mindset for winners, but that may not be enough. Positive people can also encounter failures but because of their positive attitude, they bounce back and become winners.

But having a 'strategic mindset' is very different. When you have a strategic mindset, you think very deeply and differently; you don't take your own planning for granted; you are ready to adjust (not compromise) and you start working towards your goals.

In this book, we are going to explore all the time-tested principles of the 'art of winning' in 'the Chanakya way'.

As we start to explore Chanakya's teachings together, let me ask you a very important question: how important is winning in life?

Take a pause for a few moments and think about it. I can also rephrase the question and ask: how important is winning in life for *you*?

The 'you' is very important here. If 'you' decide to win, nothing can stop you. But if 'you' decide not to win, you will lose, even if victory comes knocking at your door. So, think carefully and answer the question. If winning is important in life for you, only then can others help you. It always starts with your personal mindset.

Henry Ford, the founder of Ford motors and one of the most successful businessmen of American history, said something very profound: 'If you believe you can, or if you believe you cannot—either ways you are right.' Therefore, if you have decided to be a winner, this book will teach you the art of winning.

◆

Chanakya took a lot of time to choose his best student whom he wanted to make the emperor of India. He finally found the true makings of a king in Chandragupta Maurya and trained him in the art of winning. He also gave him a reference or training manual called *Arthashastra*. It is a ready reckoner that one can use to aid themselves in any given situation.

In *Arthashastra*, Chanakya calls his student *Vijigishu*—a person who wants to conquer the world and become numero uno. (If we were ever told that Indians never wanted to be world conquers, it is not true.) But here, conquering does not merely imply killing or destroying. That is a very non-Indian method. You can win through strategy, careful planning and perfect execution. To reach one goal, you may have multiple paths or methods. Among others, you may know about *Sama, Dana, Danda* and *Bheda*, which were proposed by Chanakya to win over the competitor.

Whatever field you may be from, you can use this book to become a winner: in sports, business, politics, at home, in your career or even in the spiritual field. Use this book as your guide to winning and making others winners as well.

Now coming back to my question: how important is winning in life? Yes. It is very important to be a winner in life. Who does not like to win, right? No one wants to be a failure.

Winning is a great feeling. The thought of victory itself makes us feel confident and drives us to do better each time. It makes us feel enthusiastic. It energizes us. And winning leads to more winning. It is contagious. If you are a winner, you can create more winners. They inspire others. People like to get associated with winners. They admire winners and want to be like them. This is the power of winning.

Each one of us is born to win; no one is born to fail. Winning is our birth right. Of course, let us not use the wrong methods to win. Let us be honest in our purpose. Let us not cheat others. When we are talking about strategy, we are not talking about manipulation. We can be slow but sure in moving towards our purpose.

When we look back at our wins, we should feel proud of them and not become arrogant with our victory. We should be gentle and humane after winning too. In the end, we will realize that true winners are gentle and soft inside. Their determination is not about destruction. They love to create and leave a legacy.

Let us all be such 'ideal' winners whom generations to come would admire and emulate. And not just winning lessons, but life lessons. The way you respected, admired and treated others with love and compassion is always remembered. Win you must, but through the right means; win you should, by taking others along and win you can, through *Art of Winning: The Chanakya Way*.

1

THE WINNING MINDSET

You can conquer the world. But first, you
will have to conquer the fear inside you.

—Chanakya

Everything begins with the mind. If we are able to understand the mind and how it functions, we will have a winning advantage over others. If we control the mind, we can win the world.

This implies that the mind is continuously active. It is thinking something or the other; it cannot stop or be still, even when one is asleep. We call thoughts we have while sleeping 'dreams'. At times, negative thoughts and images turn into nightmares. Some people who have sleep disorders cannot control their minds and thoughts and, at times, professional involvement and medical intervention are required. Psychiatrists, psychologists, counsellors and philosophers come to help us to understand how to deal with our mind.

In recent years, along with physical health, people are taking 'mental health' very seriously. Problems such as depression, stress, mental burnout and other disorders of the mind have become a special branch of research and study. Today, there is also a lot of research being done in the field of cognitive sciences, where the thoughts of a person are studied in detail to understand better functioning of the mind.

We are living in a strange era. World over, thinkers and leaders are working on making the world a better place by ensuring adequate food, clothing, shelter and other basic facilities for all. But new problems of the mind that are emerging, which governments have to deal with, require raising concerns about suicides, lack of focus and concentration, loneliness, etc.

Now come two interesting questions for us. In India, in the past, have we faced problems related to the mind? And if so, did our ancestors find some practical solutions for such mental health problems?

The answer to both the questions is a big, resounding yes.

What we consider modern-day challenges have been present throughout human history. Every generation has tried to understand the mind and bring some solutions to the challenges related to the mind and its functioning. Particularly in the Indian culture, having the right state of mind, called *Mana-sthiti* in Sanskrit, is important to face various situations (*Paristhiti*). So, if your mind is under control, the situation can also be easily controlled. And one of the practical tools our rishis (sages) developed to control the mind is meditation. Yes, meditation is India's greatest gift to the world. We taught the world to meditate, keep the mind focused and, through concentration and strategy, take the right decision. Now the question arises: how does the control of the mind lead to a winning mindset?

The Chanakya Story

Once, Chanakya was sitting quietly in his gurukul. He was in deep thought when one of his students approached him and asked, 'Guruji, what exactly are you thinking?'

Chanakya turned around to face the student. There was an expression of calmness and serenity on the face of the teacher. And, still in deep thought, he said, 'There are two worlds that all of us simultaneously live in: the internal world and the external world.

'Most of us spend a lot of time preparing to win in the external world. But the reality is different. We need to first prepare to win inside. Before we conquer the outer world, we need to conquer our inner world. If you are a winner inside, it is easy to win outside. Therefore, I am sitting here and creating a winning mindset in me.'

The student was thrilled by what his guruji had just said and wanted to know more about creating this winning mindset. 'Can you teach us how to create this winner inside us?' he asked, eagerly.

Chanakya took a deep breath and said, 'I can do that. But you will have to *learn* it. Remember, strategy is not taught; it is caught. So, you have to catch it when I teach it. Today, in my class, I will teach you how to create this winning mindset. So please pay attention.'

Later that day, Chanakya, in his strategy class, said, 'Today, I am going to give all of you a practical challenge. I will be happy if you can succeed in it.'

The students looked at each other. They knew that their teacher had many methods to test his students. This seemed to be one of those 'surprise tests' for them.

Chanakya continued to explain, 'I will be sending you

to the jungle tonight. You all have to go to the other side of the jungle. There is a small village there, and in the village temple, there is a priest. You have to go and meet him and ask for the temple jewellery. Then, you have to come back to me with that jewellery, and hand it over to me.'

The students started to plan their visit to the temple in their minds, and as they were doing it, Chanakya added, 'But, my dear students, let me add something as a caution. The jungle is not safe. It is full of wild animals. On the route, there are many man-eating tigers. You will have to stay in the jungle for two nights. One night while going and the other night while coming back. So, you have to be very careful.

'Also, let me warn you that the temple priest is a very rough person. He will not allow you to touch his temple jewellery. And he dislikes me a lot. So, if you tell the priest that you are my students, he will hate you. To sum up, it is not easy to get the temple jewellery. The jungle route is dangerous and the priest will not support you at all.'

The students then started to think differently. They started wondering about how to be safe in the jungle, how to negotiate with the temple priest, how to plan the return journey to the gurukul and so on.

Chanakya further added, 'Remember this rule: you cannot fight with the priest or argue with him, neither steal the temple jewellery. Also even if you get the jewellery by any means, you will also face some robbers on the way. Be wary of them stealing it from you.'

While the students were contemplating the challenges they would be facing in this task, their guruji continued, 'Also note that you cannot carry any food or water with you. And the jungle has many poisonous fruits in it, so you will have to be very careful. And there are hardly any water sources there.'

The students started getting worried. Chanakya continued, 'If you come back alive, that itself will be a great achievement, let alone bring back the temple jewellery.'

And then he asked the students, 'How many of you want to take this risk of going to the other side of the jungle and probably not come back, and how many want to take up another challenge instead?'

The students were very happy to know that they had other options as well.

'Another option is staying back in the gurukul itself and making some carvings. It has to be made out of the wood that is kept aside for building statues.'

As this was a very easy challenge to take up, most of the students decided to avoid going through the jungle and its difficulties. Finally, only three students agreed to take up the jungle challenge. And thus, there were two sets of students: the ones who would go into the jungle and the ones who would make the best of carvings while staying back in the gurukul.

Chanakya then addressed the three students who had decided to go into the jungle. 'All of you have to go separately. Not as a group. In case you feel frightened, come back soon. Nothing to worry at all.'

The three students took the blessings of their teacher and started towards the jungle. Their task was to be completed within three days and they were to report to Chanakya thereafter. Meanwhile, the remaining students stayed in the campus and started to make the carvings.

The three students started the journey separately on the same day, and by afternoon one student came back. He rushed towards Chanakya and said, 'No, Guruji, no. I think I made a mistake by taking up the other challenge. Can I request to choose carving the sculpture instead?'

'Of course,' Chanakya replied. 'That is your choice. Welcome back. And you start working on your carvings.'

By the same evening, another student who had gone to the jungle rushed back towards the gurukul, running very fast as he wanted to reach before sunset.

As soon as he reached the gurukul, he said, 'Guruji, I cannot face the dark and wild animals, so I came back. Can I join the others in making the carvings?'

'Most welcome,' said Chanakya.

The night had arrived. Now, only one student remained outside the gurukul.

All were worried, that he may be killed. Without any food to eat and water to drink, how will he survive the night?

The second day too passed and so did the second night. The students were getting increasingly worried as there was no communication at all. At the same time, they were busy preparing their best carvings.

And finally, the third day arrived. The afternoon passed, and it was soon to be evening. The other students had almost completed their assignments of making the wooden carvings. They were eagerly waiting to show them to their teacher. Still, there was no sign of the student who had gone into the jungle. The rest of the students were sure that he was killed in the attempt of getting the temple jewellery. But as the sun began to set, they saw, at a distance, the student walking back towards the gurukul. As he came closer, they saw that he was happy and smiling. He also had a small, neatly covered bag tugged in this arm.

As soon as he entered the gurukul, he touched his

teacher's feet and said, 'Guruji, here is the jewellery you wanted.'

All the remaining students were surprised at the achievement. They could not believe it at all.

Chanakya took the jewellery and blessed the victorious student. The others asked him, 'How was the journey through the jungle, the stay, the experience with the temple priest?'

The student smiled at his guru and said, 'It was the smoothest journey I have ever had. As soon as I entered the jungle, there was a man who came to me. I was very afraid as it was getting dark, and I thought he was a robber. But surprisingly, he said he had been sent by our Guru Chanakya. He was supposed to take care of any students who came here.

'He took me to his house inside the jungle and gave me fresh food, which was very tasty. I slept very well without any problems. In the morning, I took a bath and went ahead. Very soon, I crossed the jungle and reached the village.

'The temple priest also welcomed me. He said that he was waiting for someone to come, so that he could hand over the temple jewellery. This was to be sent to Guru Chanakya.

'He also offered me food and other resting facilities. Then, as I started on my journey back, the priest advised his son to come with me so that the jewellery would be safe.

'As soon as I returned to the jungle again, the same person was waiting for me. I spent one more night at his house. I was very well taken care of. And look, I am back with the jewellery as advised by our guru, Acharya Chanakya.'

All the children heard this tale in shock, while the student who had chosen to undertake the challenge in the jungle looked at a smiling Chanakya and asked, 'Guruji, you had said that there would be a lot of problems on the way: wild animals, no food, the unfriendly priest and many other things. But everything was just the opposite...'

Chanakya replied, 'I was actually testing all of you by creating imaginary problems that never really existed.'

The students then realized that it was a plot created by their teacher. Chanakya continued to explain, 'I deliberately infused fear into your mind and all of you accepted that as reality. Everything was prearranged. I had already organized for one of my students to receive you inside the jungle. His duty was to take care of you. The priest is a friend of mine and was ready with the jewellery. At every step, it was safe and secure.

'Yet, I wanted you all to take the first step. The rest was already taken care of. Most of you did not take even the first step, imagining the problems ahead. Three of you started but two of you came back. It is only one student who actually took the first step inside the jungle, and he ended up having to do nothing. The moment you entered the jungle, you had already emerged as a winner. Congratulations!'

Chanakya then explained what he was trying to teach them. 'Winning starts with creating a winning mindset. There are three types of people: the first kind never start, imagining the problems ahead; the second kind start, but the moment they face a problem, they turn back and the third kind keep walking, face the problems and emerge as winners.'

The students realized that the path they had chosen determined the kind of people they were.

Chanakya continued, 'Most of the times, there are no problems. If there are any, they are self-created. It is very simple: we complicate it through our imagination.

'So, my dear students, always keep your mind focused on the goal rather than keeping your focus on the challenges and problems. You need to win over imagined fears in the beginning itself: this is the winning mindset.'

In conclusion to his lesson, he said, 'What is fear? Fear is just another thought that comes to your mind. Most of the time, the things you fear are only in your imagination, not real. Be watchful of your thoughts. Kill the unnecessary ones before they overwhelm you. Winning over fear is the first step to overall victory.'

Chanakya Neeti

You can conquer the world. But first,
you will have to conquer the fear inside you.

—Chanakya

The concept of Vijigishu is given in *Arthashastra*. A Vijigishu is a person who wants to be a world conqueror. Chanakya helps his students to prepare them in becoming Vijigishus or winners at a global level.

However, one often does not realize that being number one does not mean you will have to kill and loot others. You can be the best by bettering yourself. If you can better yourself, every time you face a challenge, you will be a consistent winner. So, discard the fear of losing. Fear is dangerous. Let it not form at all. As soon as you realize its presence, nip it in the bud. Only then will you emerge as a winner.

While it is natural for us to have fear inside us, the

continuation of that fear depends on us. Take fire, for instance. When we see fire, we have a natural instinct to get away from it. But if we start fearing it, we will not be able to use the fire well. If we can control the fire, we will reap its benefits.

Let us take this example to an extreme: suppose there is a house on fire. Naturally, anyone would instinctively be fearful of an inferno. But we have to pause and think: if we run away like others, we will be safe. But there is no guarantee that the fire will be put out. So, we should take a deep breath and instead of fear taking over our minds, analyse the situation, think what can be done to put off the fire and a calm and quiet mind will help us arrive at solutions.

We may think of calling the fire department or looking for the nearest water supply or calling some friends to put out the fire. But if we run away, we can never be leaders in such situations. Therefore, the difference between a winner and a loser lies in the ability to conquer fear in the initial stages.

All successful people are able to conquer their inner fears. As soon as they see it coming, they become alert and vigilant. They watch their mind and its thoughts. Then once they are able to overcome the impulse of fear, they start finding solutions to the problem at hand. Be it business, sports, politics, school and college or the battlefield, real winners have a 'winning mindset'. And once you have this winning mindset, nothing can stop you from winning—nothing.

Friends, now visualize a situation where something challenging or fear inducing comes before you. In such a situation, stop thinking too much. Take a deep breath and allow the fear in you to settle down. Watch your mind and you will be surprised at how solutions emerge by themselves, automatically giving you access to the 'winning mindset'.

Chanakya's Practical Tips

What Chanakya Says

1. The most important quality of winners is that they always focus on the end result. They know exactly what they want: it is crystal clear in their minds. Therefore, it is important to be clear about the end result you want, and then work towards achieving it.

    Therefore, one of the important aspects of winning is to do a 'goal-setting' exercise. Once the goal is set, you know what you need to focus on. If you have not done a goal-setting exercise till now, I recommend you to start from this point. If you know your goals, you will achieve them.

2. One of the biggest hurdles in the journey of being a winner is self-doubt. If others doubt you, it is fine. That is something you cannot control. If others don't believe in you, do not worry about convincing them. Once you become a winner, they will naturally appreciate you. But there is no remedy for self-doubt. You have to tell yourself to think like a winner. Never doubt yourself.

    Once, a disabled person was trying to crawl up a mountain. A marathon runner was also running up the mountain. He said to the differently abled person, 'I don't think you will be able to reach the mountaintop. You should go back.' The differently abled person told him, 'I have already reached the top of the mountain. My body catching up is only a matter of time.'

This is the winning mindset: no self-doubt, even if others create a doubt in your mind. This is confidence in yourself, your ability and your willpower. No power in the world can stop people who have decided to be winners.

3. It is quite possible that even when you have developed a winning mindset, you may not know the game well. You may be doing business for the first time, you may be in a new country or you may be playing a sport for the first time. In such a situation, do not worry if the game is new to you. Seek advice of experts in such a case. Along with a winning mindset, create a 'learner's mindset'; then, it is easy for you to win the game. Learn the rules of the game through the experts and you will emerge a winner.

Remember the movie *Lagaan*, where the hero Bhuvan (Aamir Khan) had a winning mindset but no experience in the game of cricket? He had accepted the challenge of the British team to win against them in the game of cricket but did not know how to play cricket.

That did not matter. Bhuvan also had a learner's mindset. He learnt the game with the help of others who knew how to play cricket. And, finally, with the team Bhuvan managed to create and with his leadership attitude, they all emerged winners in front of a more powerful team.

Winning begins within you. Prepare yourself internally first, and you can become winners externally.

All the best for creating *the winning mindset*!

POINTS TO REMEMBER

1. Focus on the result. Bearing the goal in the mind, we will not lose track.
2. Do not doubt yourself. Trusting yourself is the key to success; self-confidence will take you forward every time you are stuck.
3. Seek advice. When you do not know what to do, seek the advice of experts who will show you the way forward.

2

WHO IS YOUR REAL FRIEND AND WHO IS YOUR RIVAL?

*Test before you trust. And continuously
test those whom you trust.*

—Chanakya

Our experiences are our greatest teachers. Life teaches us a lot. Sometimes during our struggles—when we need support the most, friends might not be there for us. And sometimes, help comes in the form of the most unexpected people. After all, a friend in need is a friend indeed. Clichéd, but true. Life is unpredictable in this way. All of us have felt cheated by someone or the other: someone you trusted must have broken your trust. However, someone you hated could have turned out to help you in the most difficult times.

However, imagine a situation where you are able to judge the other person right from the very beginning. You recognize the attitude of the person from day one. You will then not get cheated; you will be alert and turn out a winner in every situation. But how do you know who is your real friend and who is your rival? This knowledge is one of the most important aspects of being a winner.

At the end of the day, victory comes with teamwork, and having the right allies and partners on your side is the key to success. If you get wrong people to partner with, you will get cheated in the end. But if you get the right people as your partners, you will not only win in the end but also will be happy and share the joy of winning. This is where Chanakya's wisdom to understand human psychology works. He knew exactly who his potential friends and enemies were, even when disguised.

As the mind, so the person. Once you have an understanding of the other person, their thoughts and feelings, their value systems and objectives in life, you can easily judge the person. Then you will have to check your compatibility with them. If you are compatible, you have high chances of succeeding; if not, then the chances are reduced significantly. No wonder choosing your life partner is one of the toughest decisions one makes in their life.

The Chanakya Story

Chanakya's life was full of adventures, challenges and achievements. When he was a child, King Dhana Nanda of the Nanda Dynasty that ruled the Magadha Empire had killed his father Chanak, as he had created a public uprising against the corrupt practices of the king. Chanakya had to flee from Pataliputra, the capital of Magadha, to Takshashila in order to save his life. At Takshashila, he studied various schools of thoughts of Arthashastra and himself became a prominent acharya or teacher. After he excelled as both a student and a teacher of political science and economics, he had to return to Pataliputra. He dethroned Dhana Nanda and made one of his students, Chandragupta Maurya, the emperor of united India. During the same time, he also defeated Alexander the Great, who was on his way to conquer the world, through his strategies. Later, Chanakya started documenting his life-long experiences and wrote his own version of *Arthashastra*, popularly known as *Kautilya's Arthashastra*.

Name, fame, popularity, money, power—all followed Chanakya. But he did not get carried away by all these. He wanted to be a simple teacher and pass on his knowledge and wisdom to his students. He knew that being a kingmaker was better than being a king. Simple yet sharp, humble yet intelligent—Chanakya's name spread far and wide. Every day, he had visitors from different parts of the country and also from across the globe. He was a man of achievement and everyone took his advice. Anyone who came to Chanakya would get more than they expected through the pearls of wisdom he had to share. All his friends, including his childhood friends, were proud of him and they took pride in telling others, 'Yes, Chanakya is our dear friend. We have known him since childhood.'

Chanakya was at the peak of glory at this point in his life. Most important people used to come to him to learn and discuss about the ideas he had written in *Arthashastra*.

Once, Chanakya was meditating in his gurukul when his childhood friend arrived. They had studied together in their younger days, and the other friend also had become a teacher of political science or *Raja Niti*, like Acharya Chanakya himself. They met regularly and discussed matters concerning the kingdom, political scenarios, economic situations and global challenges, and in the discussions, both friends learned a lot from each other.

As soon as Chanakya's meditation was over, he got up and received his friend with a warm hug. Both friends loved to have long talks devoid of any selfish, ulterior motives. But from time to time, they used to have serious discussions about their duty as teachers to society. At a serious moment in this particular instance, Chanakya's friend commented, 'Vishnu, you have become a world-famous person, thanks to your strategies.'[1]

This friend of Chanakya asked out of concern and curiosity, 'Vishnu, all types of people come to you. From emperors to common men, from teachers, traders and merchants to the directionless youth. With such a variety of visitors, how do you know who is your real friend and who is your rival?'

Chanakya smiled and agreed, 'That is so true, my dear friend. All types of people come to me and I have to give audience to all of them. I never deny meeting anyone. Our Indian culture says *Atithi Devo Bhava:* even a visitor without an appointment should be considered as god.

'But then, one cannot be undiscerning when we meet anyone, especially strangers. We have to be smart and judge the person and his intentions. If you are unable to judge correctly, there is a big chance that they can misuse your popularity and fame.'

---

[1]Chanakya had three names: Vishnugupta, his childhood first name given by his parents; Kautilya, the name he used while writing *Arthashastra* and Chanakya because he was the son of Acharya Chanak, a great political scientist and teacher. Most of Chanakya's friends used to call him Vishnu, the short form of Vishnugupta. Though he was very popular as Chanakya, he loved to be called Vishnu by his friends.

Chanakya's friend understood that Chanakya, though open to meeting and keeping an open door for everyone, was extremely sharp while dealing with different types of visitors.

He continued to quiz him, 'But then how do you know the intentions of the people who come to you, that too when they meet you for the first time?'

Chanakya smiled again. 'That is the key to success and winning in life. If you can understand the intentions of the person, then you know how to deal with them.'

He further explained, 'I put all visitors under two categories: one consisting of people who knew me before I became famous and the other consisting of people who come to me because of my fame. Usually the ones who come to me due to my fame have some agenda or intention. I judge that pretty early and never allow them to take me or my knowledge for granted. The second category is the people who have known me before I became famous. I know they are my real friends for life. They do not have any selfish intentions. I am safe and secure with such friends and do not fear sharing my knowledge and wisdom with them.'

Placing his hands on the shoulder of his childhood friend, Chanakya smiled and said, 'I have no threat from you. You have no wrong intentions. You are my genuine friend. Come, it is time for lunch. Let us continue our discussion after partaking our food.'

Chanakya Neeti

It is not easy to recognize the difference between friends and enemies. Sometimes friends appear to be enemies, and sometimes enemies seem like friends. A number of factors are involved in every relationship. Circumstances and situations matter a lot, and depending on certain parameters, things can change overnight. So, in order to be a winner in life, we need to take this into account. It is not suggested that you start doubting your friends and consider them as potential enemies or start trusting your enemies overnight. The suggestion is to be aware and flexible while dealing with people. If you have to trust someone, do that. But remember this *Chanakya Neeti,*

> *Test before you trust. And continuously*
> *test those whom you trust.*

Trust is a very delicate thing. If you trust too much, there is a fear of being cheated. At the same time, if you do not trust, you cannot work in this world. It is a Catch-22 situation. You cannot do without it, nor can you avoid it. Therefore, to handle such situations, you need to be very careful and alert.

Do not become a doubting Thomas, a kind of person who keeps doubting everyone around them. Such people do not trust anyone at all. They are sceptics, who refuse to believe anyone. In fact, if one continues this habit, it can become a psychological problem and even become your attitude in life. It is a dangerous mental trap that can have plenty of negative implications.

At the same time, we have also heard about cases where one had trusted someone blindly and had to pay a heavy price for it. These may include a friend one had issued a blank cheque to, only to find that that friend cheated you or a caretaker who betrayed your trust by robbing the house in your absence. It is fine when such things happen in the early stages of a relationship. But what if this happens after trusting a person over a period of time and they cheat you after 20 years of having a relationship?

So, what does one do? Do not worry. Chanakya has a solution for every such case. Let us look again at the *Chanakya Neeti* mentioned earlier.

The first part says 'Test before you trust'. This is already done in most organizations while recruiting new employees. There are various rounds of testing that are undertaken before hiring. Backgrounds, referrals and recommendations—all of these are checked. At times, a person is also sent home to check if all the information given is authentic and true.

Take, for example, the armed forces. When they are recruiting their officers or soldiers, a high level of testing is done. They start with the physical tests like running, medical tests and other such exams. Next comes the written test, where the intellectual abilities are tested. And finally, there is a personal interview, where questions are asked.

Interviews are actually methods of finding out many qualities of a person, including situational analysis, decision-making ability and leadership skills, among others. Based on the outcomes of all these tests, they are finally given an appointment letter to join the organization.

However, for a new person, there is a probation period. This is also a kind of a testing period that lasts anywhere between three months and three years. Someone on probation is under the supervision of a well-experienced person, and once the person demonstrates that they can do the tasks well in the probation period, only then is the person given a permanent position in the organization, i.e. their services are confirmed.

Chanakya was the first to start such formal recruitment process in the government machinery. In *Arthashastra*, written in the fourth century BC, about 2,400 years ago, he mentions how a person should be tested for a ministerial position. In Book 2 of *Arthashastra*, in the chapter 'Amatya Utpatti' (Creation and Selection of a Minister), Chanakya mentions various tests for a minister. Those who are interested in knowing more can study the original work in Sanskrit to get a deeper understanding of the subject.

However, the amount of time spent in an organization or a person's seniority cannot be a definite measure of a person's trustworthiness. We have also seen cases of able people in senior-management positions indulging in corruption and malpractices. This is where the second part of *Chanakya Neeti* comes in: 'Continuously test the person whom you trust'. Organizations do that through various means like audits (both internal and external), reports, management information systems (MIS) and performance appraisals.

If we do not test continuously, people end up taking things for granted: they will not be serious about their work, and the danger is that slowly, a sense of lethargy and non-performance can set in, which will lead to financial losses and stagnation. Continuous tests, the feeling that one is responsible for the work given and the fear of non-performance leading to job loss keep everyone alert and on their toes, thus enhancing performance.

On a personal level, both at work and outside, we should test everyone to develop trust. After we establish trust with a person, we should also test the person from time to time. This is not being a doubting Thomas, but being practical, realistic and not allowing anything to be taken for granted.

To be a winner in life you should know who your real friends and opponents are. Let us now look at steps to find our friends and foes.

Chanakya's Practical Tips

What Chanakya Says

In order to win, we should clearly know who our friends and enemies are. With friends, we partner; with enemies, we fight. Real friends should be our partners and allies, and we should be very careful with our enemies.

Never take your friends or enemies for granted. If you take friends for granted, they will not like you and may not support you when you need them the most. If you take your enemies for granted, they will defeat you easily. So, let us look at some practical tips to find out who your real friends and enemies are.

1. The first step to test before you trust is to never assume things as they appear on their first impression. It is true that first impressions are lasting impressions. However, we need to verify it against the information available about the person in question. There is a saying, 'Your reputation goes before you.' Any person's reputation is already built beforehand and it is important to check that reputation.

    In today's generation, it is easy to check a person's background: you can check his social media accounts. Through Facebook, Twitter, LinkedIn or Instagram, you can gather a lot of information about a person like where they spend their maximum time, their friend circle, their interest areas, educational qualifications and job experience.

One important thing to remember while checking the background is 'birds of a feather flock together'. This means that we should also check the background of the people with whom the person in question spends the maximum time with, personally and professionally.

And finally, it is also imperative to check the family background of the person. This is very critical in determining if a person is trustworthy or not as we can easily understand the upbringing and the value systems of the person. A person from a business family will already have an understanding of business practices and a person who comes from a highly educated family will have a similar background.

2. We must always remember that everything that glitters is not gold. When we are doing a background check on a person, especially on social media, we are not going to come across their darker side as they may not have put it up on their public profiles. No one wants to reveal their true colours. We need to verify the existing information with people who really know the person.

Therefore, the best way of testing a person is asking the people who have worked with them. Such people know the person's behaviour, attitude, aptitude and capability. We should check with their real friends, bosses and family members to get deeper and detailed information.

Next, we need to think ahead. Simply gathering information and verifying it is not what needs to be done: our real objective is to work with the person and find success in the joint partnership. Unless our main job is policing and investigation, we need to take the next concrete steps to start working with the person.

Initially, we should not jump into a big project together, especially when we are working with the person for the first time. We should try something small first, and if it succeeds, then we can take bigger strides. This is called working on a 'pilot project'. Once the project finds its success, one can scale it up. It is like trying a sample before we buy the new product. It is fine if we do not like the sample product; we need not buy the product. A pilot project is like an engagement period before marriage takes place. In the duration of the engagement, a couple tries to understand each other better, come to know each other's habits and behaviour patterns and, once compatibility is found, the marriage will be a success.

3. It is important in relations with others to keep communicating regularly. If we do not do that, there are dangers of being cheated as well. When we communicate on a regular basis, there is a lot of information that gets conveyed. If the other person does not communicate, we should seek information and communication from them. If not, we will not understand what is going on in the other person's mind. Among friends and family, we keep asking how they are and what they are doing. If there is

a communication gap, we may not understand the changes the person goes through.

This is how Chanakya maintained his relationships: he continually gathered information about his friends and foes. This happened through his spy systems, surprise checks, internal audit mechanisms and other such methods. Once we do that on a regular basis, we get a feel of how the person is. Then we can decide who our real friends are and who our enemies are. Many a time, we find that a so-called friend is passing on our information to the enemy camp. The enemy may have even planted one person inside our camp. The seeming friend may be an enemy in reality.

One very interesting way to judge a person is how they deal with financial matters. A true friend is always trustworthy when it comes to money, but an enemy will cheat us in financial matters whenever they get an opportunity. Keeping an eye on our financial transactions with the other person could reveal a lot about the person's character. That is the reason why Chanakya wrote *Arthashastra*, a scripture on wealth. Money is power, and in friendship or in enmity, if money comes into the picture, the game changes completely. This is why it is important to get our finances right—to easily distinguish between a real friend or a potential enemy. Money is where the power game begins.

If you want to be a winner in life, make sure you understand the person and their attitude towards money and power.

POINTS TO REMEMBER

1. Do a background check. It is important to check the background of the people who you are dealing with.
2. Engage in a pilot project. Start everything with a pilot project and then learn from it before embarking on a big project.
3. Regular communication is the key to success.

3

KNOWING YOUR RIVALS: THEIR STRENGTHS AND WEAKNESSES

The affairs of a king [leader] are [of three kinds, namely] directly perceived, unperceived and inferred.

—Chanakya

Your rivals are your competitors, so you should be aware of them. You should know their strengths and weaknesses. If you do not take cognizance of them, your business will be taken over by them. Usually, your rivals would be of two types: direct competitors and indirect competitors. Mostly, you only plan for a strategy over direct competitors. However, that is not a good strategy at all as, sometimes, your indirect competitors can take over you.

Let us first understand what is meant by direct and indirect rivals or competitors. Direct competitors are the ones you can see face to face, those who are in front of you. You are aware of them and will always plan your competitive strategies against them. Indirect competitors are those you do not see directly. They may be smaller than you in size, but if you take them lightly, they will defeat you easily. They sometimes shock you and, at times, they also defeat you.

Let us take a few examples to understand the difference

between direct and indirect rivals. Suppose you are in the publishing industry. Your direct competitor could be other newspapers or book publishing houses. However, your indirect competitors would be digital and electronic publishing. They would compete with you indirectly as, today, news on websites and e-books is becoming very popular and magazines are also available in electronic formats. For a small kirana or grocery store in your locality, direct competition would be another kirana store in the same locality, but indirect competition would come from departmental stores and supermarkets. Today, e-commerce and online shopping are very popular as well. Those who are smart and can identify different types of competition will always reign supreme as winners. When you build your strategy against your rivals, you must build it keeping in mind your direct and indirect competition.

When Facebook was doing very well, it found that there were other similar social media platforms that were taking away their market share. Through deeper research, they identified that one of the upcoming competitors was WhatsApp. Facebook knew that over a period of time, WhatsApp could outgrow Facebook subscriptions and their business model could be negatively impacted. So, what do you think Facebook did? It bought WhatsApp! It was acquired for US$19 billion. It is one of the largest acquisitions till date. One may wonder if this was important. Only time proved that it was the right decision. One of the most valued companies in the world is Google. It realized the sudden growth of YouTube in the search engine space. The free video streaming model of YouTube was not taken as direct competition by many. But Google took over YouTube, and today, it is a subsidiary company of Google.

There are methods to know who your direct and indirect competitors are, so that you can prepare your strategies around them.

The Chanakya Story

Chanakya believed that one of the first steps in knowing a rival is gathering information about them. He used to have a network of spies in place to collect information for him. He would then analyse the situation and take necessary action against the rivals. He had also created an espionage mechanism, which is mentioned in the fourth volume of *Kautilya's Arthashastra*.

Chanakya also had a special team of women spies called *Vishkanyas* (the women of poison). They would go into the enemy camp, entice the enemy and kill them through different methods. This is also called 'honey trap' in the modern era. In the field of military strategy and intelligence gathering, this is very common. Here is one such story of Vishkanyas.

Chanakya knew that women always had a different view and an alternative method of thinking. One of Chanakya's strengths was the ability to grasp this different viewpoint. He could decode some of the most difficult situations and complex problems using inputs given by women.

To gather the right information from the camp of Alexander the Great, he had sent Vishkanyas into his camp. They went into the army barracks and gathered the required information. When they came back, he asked them, 'Tell me in detail about what is happening inside the camp of Alexander.'

They described in detail the camp settings, the strength of the army, their weapons and other various set-ups within the camp. They often overheard military strategies being discussed, which they shared with Chanakya. He listened to their inputs with rapt attention and said, 'Thank you for the information. I am already aware of the information that you shared with me. There is nothing new. Give me an input that will make a strategic difference.'

Chanakya was not only trying to know his rivals or their strengths and weaknesses; he wanted to find some differentiating factor that would make a big difference, something very 'insightful'. Therefore, he sent them back saying, 'Go observe them properly.'

The Vishkanyas went back to the enemy camp and observed Alexander's army in greater detail. They then came back to Chanakya and reported, repeating more or less the same information that they had gathered previously. They went into the detail of describing the colour of their dresses, food habits, kitchen occurrences and daily time tables, among others.

Again Chanakya said, 'I want something more. Go back again and investigate deeply. I want you to see something that is not visible easily, something very different, something that could be a game changer. Try and read in between the lines. Try and look into their eyes: eyes can reveal more about a person than anything else. They are the true window to a person's heart.'

The Vishkanyas went back to the enemy camp for the third time. This time, a young girl went into the camp with a different approach. She did as advised by Chanakya. When she came back, Chanakya asked her, 'How was the experience this time? Any new input for me?'

The girl said, 'Acharya, if you can demoralize the soldiers of the army, they all will go back home. You do not have to fight a battle at all.'

'What do you mean by that?' he asked, surprised at the unusual input.

The girl responded saying, 'As stated by you, I looked into the eyes of the soldiers and found something interesting. I found that they were very homesick; they were tired. These soldiers were large in size and very cruel. They could massacre a whole city without even thinking twice. But when I looked at them, I could feel that there was a humane side to them. I could even feel a sense of being lost in their eyes. They have been fighting, plundering and killing for several years. They have become very brutal, as if bereft of feelings. Yet, I could see the longing in them, longing to be home.'

And the spy girl made a very interesting point: 'I looked at them, and they looked at me. I was initially very frightened of them. But I could see that there was an emotion of care and sadness in their eyes. Instead of looking at me as a young girl who could be their object of lust, I found them to harbour fatherly feelings for me. They miss their families and are homesick after so many years of fighting and being away from home. They want to be reunited with their families.'

Chanakya's eyes lit up. 'My girl, excellent! You have given the most important tip, something that I desperately needed. I know exactly what will work with the Greek Army. You are right. They want to go home.'

Chanakya now made a very interesting plan. He had understood that the Greek soldiers was missing being with their families, the deep need to be with those whom you love the most. He sent more of these girls into the army camp so that they could evoke such feelings of longing in them.

Now, when Alexander wanted them to fight, they had internally lost the game. They were not interested in fighting anymore. They were tired and exhausted. The only thing they wanted to do was go home and get some sleep.

This strategy worked for Chanakya.

When Alexander asked the army to fight and conquer India, none of the soldiers found any excitement in it. Finally, Alexander gave up. They had lost the battle even before it took off. Finding themselves in the midst of a massive army with elephants and a vast cavalry, the Greeks were taken completely by surprise and overwhelmed of course. They were left with no choice but to retrace their steps.

This kind of strategy in military operations is called as psy ops, or psychological operations. It is psychological warfare to defeat the enemy using propaganda and false messages and is highly effective. Chanakya had a knack for spotting the enemy's weakness.

Chanakya Neeti

According to Chanakya, one has to develop the skill of paying attention to even the minutest details. Everything has to be thought through. You need this skill especially if you are a leader, as it is your job to brainstorm and come up with out-of-the-box solutions and fresh perspectives.

The affairs of a king [leader] are [of three kinds, namely] directly perceived, unperceived and inferred.

—*Arthashastra*, 1.9.4[2]

---

[2]It indicates the reference of the sutras given in *Arthashastra*, the original text. For example, 1.5.3 would refer to (Book 1, Chapter 5, Sutra 3). You will find the same style of citation in other parts of the book as well.

'Affairs' in this context means responsibility. Therefore, a central responsibility of a leader is to think, and think from different perspectives. Chanakya gives us three ways of thinking here: directly perceived, unperceived and inferred. Let us understand these in detail.

Directly Perceived

It is something that can be seen and understood directly. For example, we saw that the female spies sent to Alexander's camp figured out aspects that were easily noticeable such as the army's settings, various weapons, etc.

Unperceived

This is something that is not seen but it is also around. Chanakya himself had not gone into the enemy camp. The information gathered is not something he has personally seen or perceived. But he has seen the unseen through the eyes of the spies.

Inferred

Out of the three, inferred thinking is the most powerful. Inference is the ability to see what others generally miss. It requires immense analysis to come to a conclusion that others may not reach. For example, inferring that there is a fire nearby by looking at the smoke. Most of us see only the smoke, not the fire. That is a logical conclusion that we draw from our own experience.

In the story mentioned earlier, we saw how the young girl was able to infer that the Greek soldiers were homesick. Chanakya figured out a strategy around it.

Leaders are meant to keep analysing the information floating around. Today, gathering information is not really a problem. We do not have to send spies into enemy camps. Through technology and satellites, we can track our rival's every move. However, today, we face a new problem: over-information, also called information pollution. There is too much information around us, which makes it hard to discern what is true and what is not. Therefore, the real crux in decision-making involves gathering information as well as finding out what information is credible.

Now comes the real challenge—data analytics. Data is the new currency, according to management and leadership scientists. However, having data is not enough; it is just a starting point. One needs to analyse the data and derive significant conclusions from it. Through the results of the data analytics, one should be able to build a strategic plan and put it into action.

Look at big companies such Amazon, Google, Facebook, etc. What do you think they are doing? They are continuously analysing data and making strategies around their data analysis. It is quite strange that all these new companies have huge turnovers and profits, which is something many companies have not been able to achieve even over generations. They are continuously studying their customers and competitors. When they understand their customers, they will create new products and services. When they find a competitor, they will defeat them and take over them. Because of the financial power they have, it is possible for them to take over any competitor. The new-age technology companies are so powerful that one cannot even guess their impact. Let us take for instance a new-age company called Facebook. Most of us know about it and have a Facebook account. Facebook had more than 2.8 billion monthly active users in 2021.

India alone has a population of 1.3 billion. So, the number of subscriptions is almost twice the entire population of a country like India. That means it has access to nearly 250 crore people. Even with such a massive number of subscriptions, Facebook knows every single user through their profile: birthdays, photos, anniversaries, friends, places visited, family events, etc. One just talks about it and Facebook knows it.

Now let us take this example one step ahead. Every country now has a digital presence. Even the economy now is digital in nature. Today, governments have access to all your data: your bank accounts, finances, addresses, you name it. They know your movements through your mobile phones; they know your past and current locations. You cannot even imagine what the government can do with the information it has about you and me. There are both positive and negative sides to open access of this information.

Personally, I see a lot of positives. The crime rates have gone down as every criminal can be digitally tracked. The government schemes and welfare measures can directly reach citizens through the Internet. The benefits that are due to common man can now be provided. And here is exactly where the Chanakya model comes in. One can analyse these data in the right manner to build in 'good governance', which was the ultimate aim of Chanakya.

Chanakya's Practical Tips

What Chanakya Says

Let us now make a strategy to identify our competitors and rivals, both direct and indirect. Both of them require a different approach, especially in today's digital era.

1. Direct Competitors

As stated earlier, the direct competitors are the ones who are part of your industry and usually they are very close to you. There is no significant difference in the way they operate and you operate. The customers are also usually the same and, therefore, we need to be alert through these methods. For example, if you are manufacturing automobiles, you usually know who the direct competitors in the field are.

a) Your information network that can tell you about your direct competitors should have regular meetings. To begin with, your information network starts with the sales force. The sales and marketing teams are generally called the 'ears and eyes' of the company. They know the pulse of the market. The sales people regularly meet the other sales people of the competitors. So, do hear out your sales team regularly and gather market information from them.

Your customers are also very important in this endeavour. Yes, your customers can tell you more about your competitors than you think. Because both you and your competitor will approach the customer, who knows both sides of the story. Therefore, 'customer feedback' is also about market feedback and competitor feedback.

b) Do not meet your sales team and your customers only to discuss business. This is a wrong strategy. Of course you should talk business: that is the first and foremost thing. But only talking shop will not give you the other side of business. When you are open minded, there is a lot of information floating around in the marketplace that you can regularly gather and use.

Customer relationship management is a key part of business. The same thing goes in other fields also. When India used to regularly win Olympics gold medals in hockey, the competitors wondered why. They came and studied the methods and tactics used by Indian players and realized that if hockey was being played on grass, Indians would definitely win. So, they changed the rules of the game and started playing on turf rather than on grass. Ever since, it has been very difficult for India to win Olympic medals in their own national game.

2. Indirect Competitors

As stated earlier, indirect competition is more dangerous than direct competition. You never know when your indirect competition can change the game. I know of a company that used to work with banks for over 25 years. Their main job was to make cheques on behalf of the bank and send letters to the customers. It was a very good business model. Suddenly, when the banks went online, the transaction methods changed. Physical cheques were not required anymore. The company closed down.

a) The best way to find your indirect competitors is to research online. It is imperative to search for available data. Search for keywords connected to your business or industry, and to succeed in your endeavours, you need to research and gather information about the latest trends.

Another way is to be active on social media, which can be a great source of information. Twitter accounts and various hashtags will give you plenty of information about various discussions happening on the Internet. The world has become so small that sitting in one place, you can actually know what is happening in your field across the globe. At times, your indirect competitor will be sitting in some corner of the world developing a future strategy.

Disruption of strategies and plans happens in every field, and it occurs rapidly. Do not take your current business model for granted. You always have to stay ahead of the curve. Instead of being taken by surprise by the changing competitive world, you should be ahead of the competition. You need to either follow the future trends or create them.

b) As you get bigger and better in your business, it can be a very useful move to appoint a research agency. The agency will study the industry and its direct and indirect competition in detail. It can diagnose the problem and do a detailed study of the data available.

Good research agencies are also very well connected with various government policies and policymakers. They are able to understand future trends. They have various predictive models at their disposal. Their research teams are highly qualified and experienced. They may be able to not only give you information but can also help you build a plan in the future. I have been very personally involved with various research agencies, and it is quite fascinating to understand their working models. They indeed give you several 'insights' that could become game changers for the industry. It becomes important to develop a strategic plan against your rivals/competitors based on the reports of these agencies.

Let me give you a very interesting and well-known example here. The two biggest competitors in the beverage market are Coca-Cola and Pepsi. These global giants have always been competing with each other to have larger market capitalization. They keep coming up with better and better strategies. One of the biggest strategies that worked for Coca-Cola or Coke was their global tie-up with McDonald's. At every McDonald's outlet, they serve Coke and other Coca-Cola products. In retaliation, Pepsi actually went on to create their own chain of restaurants called Pizza Hut.

This is how you always stay ahead of the curve. The goal of your strategy has to be to remain ahead and the competition will always teach you the best methods for it.

I always wonder what it would have been like if Chanakya were alive today. Of course, he was one of the greatest strategist the world has ever seen. But in this Internet era, he would have been far ahead of all of us. So, let us all think about Chanakya in today's generation. Let us take the advantage of the scientific development we have and use it for better strategies to become winners. Let us all think of becoming a Chanakya in our own ways.

POINTS TO REMEMBER

1. Your information network is your strength; build on it and be well informed.
2. Meet your customers regularly. They will give you feedback on whether or not you are making the right moves.
3. Research online. Today, your information network can start with searching your competition and industry trends on the Internet.
4. When you have to play the big game, involve experts and appoint a research agency.

4

HOW TO STRATEGIZE A WIN EVERY TIME

*Sama, Dana, Danda and Bheda are the
four strategies to defeat the enemy.*

—Chanakya

Is it possible to win every time? Well, the thought itself seems a little impractical. Doesn't it? We have all heard inspirational quotes such as 'winning and losing are part of life', 'ups and downs are part of life's journey', among others. If failures and losses are such an integral part of our journey and life story, how is it possible to emerge a winner every time? Or rather, is that even possible?

As surprising as it may sound, the answer to the above question is 'yes'—yes, it is indeed possible to come out a winner every time. And that is exactly what we will try to learn in this chapter.

Since we are talking about winning and losing, success and failure, let us also look at the other side of the coin. Have you heard about terms such as continuous performers or consistent growth? Have you come across a person who has never lost a fight and has always come out a winner?

Yes, such people do exist, albeit in a smaller number. These are the people we should try to emulate in our lives and take leadership lessons from. They can serve as true role models, and we can and we should look for valuable life lessons and takeaways from their struggles and success stories.

Let us take a look at some real-life examples. Have you heard of people in sales who always achieve their targets? Movie producers or actors who consistently deliver super hits? Businessmen who always make profit? Students who always top their exams? Take a closer look. Yes, there are people like that around us and they should be studied and analysed. And irrespective of their area of expertise or work, they all share common patterns for their continuous success. Let us discuss these in detail.

First, they are focused and do not lose sight of their goal, whether long term or short term. They do not let distractions take the better of them. They know their strengths and weaknesses and play accordingly. And, most importantly, these 'evergreen winners' have a clear understanding of the 'right strategy' and the 'right timing'. Once you master these two aspects, you are invincible. Of course, the importance of intelligence cannot be undermined.

One such person who was a continuous winner was Chanakya himself. Yes, this man could not be defeated because for him, winning had become a habit. And as you know, it is difficult to build a habit and equally difficult to break one. Try make winning a habit. Let winning be part of your personality. Let winning be the only thought that guides you in your life and at work in particular. Once you are focused on winning, it becomes second nature.

The Chanakya Story

Chanakya was a truly gifted teacher. He resorted to various techniques and methods to impart lessons to his students and one of these was the use of board games, which were practical in nature and helped build strategic thinking among his students. One such game that he developed was Chaturaang. 'Chaturaang' means 'four parts' ('Chatur' meaning 'four' and 'Aang' meaning 'parts').

In those days, the army basically comprised four major components: chariots, horses, elephants and soldiers. Chanakya prepared a game based on these four components, which was the predecessor of what we now call Chess (C-chariots, H-horses, E-elephants and S-soldiers).

While teaching his students the art of war through this game, he used to teach them the rules first.

'Remember, both armies have equal number of players— be it the chariots, horses, elephants or foot soldiers. Each is given equal strength. Also, the moves are the same. If a solider on one side can only go straight, the same rule applies to the opponent solider as well. So, students, if the number of players are the same and so are the moves, who will finally emerge as the winner?'

The students started to discuss and some of the smart ones started answering.

'It is the understanding of the rules of the game,' said one.

'It is the experience in playing the game,' said another.

'All that is fine, dear students,' Chanakya said, smiling. 'But remember, even if you know the rules of the game or have experience playing it, the winner is the one who has a better strategy. So, strategy is the key.

'Even experienced winners can be defeated by less-experienced players in a game with the right strategy. Just knowing the rules may not suffice. So, considering everything else is constant, your strategy matters in the end. In the battlefield, it all boils down to strategic thinking.'

As the students began to reflect on what their teacher was saying, Chanakya continued, 'There is one more thing that changes the game entirely...'

The students waited with bated breath for their teacher to finish.

Raising his eyebrows, Chanakya said, 'The player who makes the first move. That is called the first mover advantage. It sets the opponent thinking. Instead of getting defensive, you are mentally free and make the other person work under pressure.

'So, remember, whenever you get a chance to play, think from all dimensions and, if possible, take advantage of that first move. Your opening move should take the opponent by surprise. And as soon as the opponent is contemplating his next move, make another unexpected move, and then another.

'Never give the advantage of allowing the opponent to think more strategically than you. Keep his moves in check. Thus, one step at a time and you emerge a winner.'

Keeping these points in mind, the students began to play the game.

'How does one apply these principles in real-life situations?' asked Chanakya, trying to test his students and their understanding of the game.

The students realized that their acharya was talking about the practical application of the game. Seeing that the students looked perplexed, Chanakya himself started to explain. 'We are going to use the principles of Chaturaang to defeat Alexander.'

Alexander was at that time on his way to conquer the world. He had started from Greece and was almost at the borders of India. He was making all the efforts to enter India and conquer it. However, Chanakya was clear that he would not allow Alexander to accomplish his mission.

'Till now we were talking about the army being equal in size and the rules being the same in a board game. It is simple! But now, what if the powers are unequal and we have to apply different rules?

'My dear students, this is where the difference between good students and practical students come through. Not all good students are successful. When faced with practical situations, they cannot think strategically. Many students are academically brilliant. They stand out as best in their class. They are the toppers. They attend all the classes, follow all the rules and even impress their teachers with their studious attitude. But the moment they are out of the gurukul, they realize the world outside is very different. That people are different. And that the same rules of the gurukul do not apply in the outside world. Therefore, the strategy has to be different. Only if you understand this practical side of the game, will you emerge successful in life.'

The students realized the pearls of practical wisdom their teacher was imparting to them.

'Alexander does not believe in our rules. He has a bigger and more powerful army. His weapons are superior. His men are immensely inspired and have a ready-to-die attitude. Plus, he is young and dynamic. India, on the other hand, is divided into sixteen regional kingdoms. We have weapons good enough for internal battles only. Our kings are selfish and only have their own interests at heart. There is hardly a leader we can look up to. In such a case, when the opponent is totally unmatched in power and attitude, what should we do?

'If we go by our rules of the game, we will be defeated. If we try to go by their rules of the game, again we are finished. No rules work here. But we still need to emerge as winners.'

With a manipulative smile, Chanakya continued, 'I know what to do in such situations. This is where my theory of winning comes into application. Please pay attention. That theory is called Sama, Dana, Danda and Bheda. Come what may, I will not allow India to be taken over by Alexander.'

Chanakya Neeti

Chanakya's Neeti or strategy is something that is very practical and useful. It has survived the test of time and is based on principles that are eternal. So, if you want to achieve victory every time, use them to build your strategies.

> *Sama, Dana, Danda, Bheda,*
> *These are the four strategies to defeat the enemy.*
>
> —Chanakya

Just as one measure does not fit all, one strategy does not work in all situations. Many a time, the reason for failure is that we assume that what worked for us in the past, will work in the future as well. Yes, indeed your past success is important to draw lessons from. That experience cannot be overlooked. However, to assume that the strategies of the past will also work in the future is a grave mistake.

There is a famous saying, 'What got you here, will not get you there.' It means that the success of your past should not become your benchmark for the future. Let us assume that you were a school topper. But once you enter college or university, the same method of studying would not work. Therefore, you will have to change your approach to studies and have a different way of planning and studying. This approach of change is called dynamic strategy. It means that you are thinking about a strategy that works in the current situation. You are dynamic and are ready to change if required.

If you play sports, you will realize what is meant by dynamic strategy. It is continuously adjusting your plan to match what the opponent is doing. Your focus should be on winning against the opponent's moves. This dynamic thinking against the opponent is called dynamic strategy.

Let us now look more closely at this four-fold strategy that Chanakya is well known for.

Sama

Sama means discussion. This is the first and the most effective problem-solving method. Some opponents are wise and intelligent. They are logical. They see that there is no point in fighting a war. It creates problems for all. War creates destruction. Many are killed and there is a huge loss of money and property. So, why fight a war at all? In such a scenario, call/meet the opponent and have a friendly discussion with them (Sama). It will be a win-win for both sides. The underlying motto of this game plan is 'live and let live', not 'survival of the fittest'.

If your opponent is ready for such a discussion, it means that he is wise and mature. In fact, you should respect such opponents. There is a saying in the armed forces, 'The best war is the one which is won without fighting.' Sama is that method where you avoid conflict in the first stage of confrontation itself. If you take a lead in such discussions, you emerge a winner, a leader. You are the one who took the initiative of holding such a formal meet to avoid a war or a conflict. However, a lot of this depends upon the opponent as well. If the opponent is not ready for peace talks, we should try the next option, and that is Dana.

Dana

Dana means financial benefits. Money is a strange thing. Everyone understands its power. So, if Sama does not work, show the opponent a financial benefit. Once the other person sees his financial gain in the situation, he will surely consider avoiding the war.

Chanakya has clearly said in *Arthashastra*, 'Wealth alone is important to become successful in this world.' Look at the Olympics, for example. It is all about competitions in different sports, between various opponents. However, there is an economic side to the games as well. Everyone gets a financial benefit from the game. The players, the organizers, the sponsors, the government and many others involved in it are able to make money out of it. The winners of course carry home a hefty cash prize too.

So, to be a winner, try to understand the psychology of money. And it is a strong factor that changes things around. However, what if the opponent still does not understand your perspective? What do you do next? Well, try the next method, Danda.

Danda

Danda means punishment. Now, the real game begins. When the opponent becomes rigid, we have to be strong. This is using force against the opponent. If the opponent is strong, we have to be stronger. Or else, we have to get allies on our side who are stronger than our opponents. Now, it is time for war. And at times, wars cannot be avoided. So, be prepared. Start doing your backward calculations. What kind of soldiers do you need? What kind of weapons and armoury would you be needing?

Hit the opponent hard, really hard. If you can defeat the enemy in the very first move, you are truly a winner. Congratulations! But what if that does not work and you do not have the muscle or military strength to defeat the enemy? No worries, Chanakya has a solution to that as well. It is Bheda.

Bheda

Bheda means creating a split. Divide and rule is the policy to be used in this context. Remember, this method requires deep strategic thinking. An organized plan. A subtle yet powerful effort. You need to study the opponent. Do a SWOT (S-strength, W-weakness, O-opportunity, T-threats) analysis of the enemy. Try and find the enemy's weak point and hit him hard right there, breaking him.

At times, it is in the very strengths of the enemy wherein lies their weakness. Try to find that Achilles heel. Can you convert that strength into weakness? The opponent should be taken by surprise when you create the split.

Think deeply for instance, if you can actually create a power game within the enemy camp. Create a rift within the opponent's team or army and they will become self-destructive. They will do your job for *you*. It is like the goal keeper hitting a goal inside his own goal post!

Whatever be the method, you should emerge the winner.

And every time the opponent or the enemy changes, you need to build a different strategy that works and makes you a winner. Remember, the best strategy is the one that wins you the game. Rest everything is simply efforts gone waste. You can either be a winner or the one with excuses. Chanakya the teacher would never accept any excuses for not winning.

What Chanakya Says

1. One of the most important aspects to be a winner is to define what winning means to you. If you are not clear on this aspect, you are simply shooting an arrow in the dark, bereft of an aim.

    Remember, each person's meaning of a win could be different. For one student, it could be topping the class and getting the first rank in academics. Another student in the same class may want to top in sports or perhaps a dance competition. Do not commit the mistake of making comparisons here.

    Only when you know your battlefield, will you be able to develop a strategy around it. You should not be applying the right strategy in the wrong field. So, if you are in cricket, the same winning rules may not apply to a game of football.

    Think through all these aspects, even before you start playing the game to win. Also, it is important to pick up the right coach or teacher. You will also have to choose the experts of that particular field for you to win.

    So, before you play the game, think if it is worth playing it. Your game could be different and better than the current one. Deciding the right game for you is the first step towards winning.

2. Now that you have understood your game, study the other players of the game. Your opponents are very important part of the game. You may be the best player of the game, but being the best is a very relative term. The moment you have a new opponent, you can get defeated very easily. Chanakya would be cautioned of any new opponent. Your opponent could be new and small, but you never know. He can take over you.

   In every game, the experienced stalwarts are defeated by young and energetic newcomers. Do not take them for granted. Also, be it old or new opponent, it is important to study them properly. Study their patterns, how they play the game and what makes them winners.

   The opponent itself will teach you a winning strategy, if you are a good learner. In today's era, it is easy to study the opponent due to easily available information. Be informed about your opponent and create your strategy around it. Investigate and find out more about your opponent. There are many people who must have studied the opponents before you. You can also partner with them to frame a strategy. They will also help you to understand the opponent better.

   When you get into the battlefield with such preparation and homework, winning becomes easy. Planning and preparation take more time than the time actually taken to win the game, thus proving true the saying that 'the more you sweat during peace times, the less you bleed during war times.'

3. Now, this is a very different, practical tip: study the judge. You must be surprised by this suggestion. Knowing the game is one thing, being the best player is another. Knowing the opponent is an altogether different

ball game and a critical part of winning.

It is said that a good lawyer knows the case, but the best lawyer knows the judge. Even if you present the case well in the courtroom, the judge is the final decision-maker. If you can impress them with your arguments and logic, the case tilts in your favour.

In every game, there is a person who understands the game and is the final decision-maker. Understanding that person's thinking can make or mar a game, it decides whether you are a winner or a loser. This key person has a subtle veto power and holds the power to change the game in your favour and against you.

Take the example of Sudha Murty, who runs the Infosys foundation and is a bestselling author. When she had completed her engineering studies and applied at the Tata group of companies, she was not given the job, as women those days did not work on the shop floor. She understood who the final judge in this matter was: the chairman of Tata group. It was J.R.D Tata during those days. She wrote to him and asked the reason for this discrimination. Tata immediately called Murty and offered her the job. This is called 'winning' even after losing the game. When you have the judge on your side, you are sure to win the game. They can bend or at times even change the rules of the game for you!

4. While playing the game, especially for the first time, there are chances of losing. If you are a new player, do not have this fear at all. Since you do not know the game, and there already are better and bigger players, they will make sure you lose. This is where your positive approach comes handy. Stay in the game. Do not give up. Consider this your entry barrier into the game. You

may lose the battle, but you will surely win the war.

Even when you start playing the game of cricket, there could be a trail ball. Consider every game with equal seriousness. However, have the approach of long-term winning rather than short-term loss. A person who had lost a game was told by the winning opponent sarcastically, 'Better luck next time.' He quickly replied, 'Who said I lost the game? I just wanted to make sure I am part of the team. So, I had already won before the game had started. As far as winning is concerned, better luck next time.'

That is what we call a winner's attitude. Even in the biggest loss, he is a winner because he always was a winner. And what many consider as losing is just a preparatory step to winning something big. When Chanakya was called upon by his senior teachers to lead the strategic war against Alexander, he was a new player in the big game. But he knew one thing—winning is most important. He built all his strategies around it. At every stage, he was a winner.

POINTS TO REMEMBER

1. Define what winning means to you. For everyone, winning has a different meaning, what is yours?
2. Study the opponent. You have to eventually win over the opponent, so study him first.
3. Study the judge. It is he who will finally be giving the verdict.
4. Long-term winning equals short-term loss. At times, you have to let go of immediate small losses for bigger wins in the future.

5

THE IMPORTANCE OF
A WELL-LAID OUT PLAN IN
WINNING

Aanvikshiki is like a guiding lamp for all knowledges.
It is a solution to all problems.

—Chanakya

If you fail to plan, you plan to fail. Planning is a lot of hard work. It requires thinking and strategy and you need to take several factors into consideration. It is deep and thorough work. It is only when you plan in the initial stages, will you understand its benefits in the long run. Therefore, planning is the very crux of winning.

Successful students plan way ahead of time. They prepare a time-table and chart out their study schedule. They do their research, get the right materials needed such as books and notes, and take the help of their teachers and even senior students. Such focussed students involve their family members and friends in the entire process of preparing for their exams, seeking their counsel and help, as and when needed. They try to emulate the good students in their class and learn their techniques. If they have doubts, they get them clarified through their teachers and subject experts. There is a lot that happens before they actually write the exams. The exam may be of three hours, but the planning and preparation happens for months and years even.

The same can be said of competitive sportspersons. Olympic medalists would vouch for that. That final result on the field is the culmination of years of planning and preparation. Had they not planned and prepared, they would not have reached that stage. And winners or champions, when they look back, they understand that it was their gruelling hard work and planning that got them to the top.

This kind of planning applies to every field. There is a saying that goes thus, 'measure twice, cut once.' This is also a kind of planning. Imagine a tailor cutting a piece of cloth without taking proper measurements. That would be a disaster. It is a shot in the dark. And it is not just about taking measurements, it is about measuring 'twice.' This is analysis and right thinking.

Stephen R. Covey, one of the world's most famous management and leadership gurus, used to guide millions of people become winners. In his classic book *The 7 Habits of Highly Effective People*, he mentions the various stages of planning.[3] One of them is being 'proactive.' Planning requires a person to be proactive. Proactivity is not just an impulsive action. It is not just an initiative. It is deep planning that a person or team does, before starting any project or activity.

And in the same book, Covey talks about one more habit

---

[3]Stephen R. Covey, *The 7 Habits of Highly Effective People: Powerful Lessons in Personal Change*, Free Press; 15th Anniversary edition (2004).

that winners have. It is called 'sharpen the saw'. Imagine, you are a wood-cutter. For you, your saw is the most important tool. If your saw itself is not sharp enough, no matter how much effort you put into cutting trees, it will not yield the desired results.

According to Chanakya, the top qualities of a winner is being intelligent and dynamic. Intelligence means planning and dynamism is all about putting that plan into action. Swami Chinmayananda used to say, 'Plan out your work, and work out your plan.' So, let us give the utmost importance to planning as part of the winning process.

The Chanakya Story

Alexander the Great was already at the borders of India. He was ready to march and conquer our huge country. Chanakya was not a king, he did not have an army of his own, but what he had was the 'power of intellect'. He knew that he had knowledge on his side. With the power of intellect and right knowledge, he could defeat any army, even Alexander's. But Chanakya also knew that to win against a very powerful leader like Alexander and a strong army such as his, it required tremendous amount of planning. Chanakya wanted to gather a lot of information about Alexander and his army, analyse the situation and then plan the right move against his opponent.

So, the first thing Chanakya did was to summon his students. For a teacher, his students are his greatest strength. He held a meeting and told them about the danger that all of them were facing. It was a national threat, a situation not to be taken lightly. After the briefing, the students decided to form their own army to fight the enemy. They were immensely inspired by their guru's vision.

Although Chanakya was pleased to see his students' fighting spirit, he told them, 'Yes, we will have to prepare ourselves for a big war. But in a war, planning is the most crucial thing. It is more critical than the actual war itself. I want to first gather maximum information about Alexander and his army. The more I know about the opponent, the better my strategy will be.'

He then formed a team of his students to act as spies. They sneaked into their opponent's camp and keenly observed everything around them: the size of the army, the number of soldiers, the weapons they used. After a careful study of their opponent and his army, they returned and reported the same to Chanakya. Based on this information, Chanakya started to plan his strategy of attack. He realized that his small army of students was not enough to defeat the huge and mighty army of Alexander the Great. He had to change his plan. He required to seek the help of other Indian kings. He went and spoke to all of them, seeking their advice. After a lot of insistence, a few kings agreed to support him. Chanakya asked the kings to send not just their armies and soldiers in huge numbers, but, also a good number of war elephants. Most of the kings were planning to send only soldiers and horses.

When they finally came face to face in combat, Alexander's army was taken by complete surprise. They were not expecting such a large army of soldiers and elephants. The war went on for days, but Alexander was eventually defeated and he had to retrace his steps. This was a massive success for India.

Post the war, Chanakya and his students were seated for a discussion. While they were celebrating their victory, they were also analysing their success and the reason behind it with their teacher. Chanakya told them that a major cause for their victory was the large number of elephants on their side. On hearing this, the students seemed confused. They did not understand the logic.

Chanakya said, 'When you had gone to spy in the camp of Alexander before the war, I was involved in competition analysis. Every bit of information you had provided me with became a part of my planning. I realized that Alexander had a large number of effective soldiers and they were better equipped in terms of weapons and the number of horses.

'However, their army was lacking in the number of elephants. That was their weak point and we had to take full advantage of this glitch. I realized that this could be our key to success. In India, elephants are very common in warfare. While in Greece, where Alexander is from, elephants are not commonly used in wars. It would be very difficult for him to face an army consisting of elephants. So, I made sure we had maximum number of elephants on our side.

'Not just the foot soldiers, even the horses were intimidated by the presence of those elephants. These soldiers and horses have not been trained to handle such huge elephants. That was their weakness. I played on our strength—the elephants. This plan really worked. Victory is ours!'

The students were very impressed by their teacher's thinking and his ability to plan in advance.

A winner needs to know the right tools to be used. This is where careful planning comes handy. You may have a number of tools at your disposal, but the right tool has to be used for the right purpose. You do not need a sword to remove a thorn in your feet. Another thorn can do the job just fine!

According to Chanakya, detailed planning needs Aanvikshiki, the science of thinking.

Chanakya Neeti

Human beings are blessed by nature. They have a skill that is unique—the ability to think. This is what makes them different from other species. We have an intellect, using which we can conquer even nature. We do not have wings, but we can make airplanes and conquer the skies. We cannot breathe underwater, but using an oxygen cylinder, we can go deep-sea diving and discover its treasures. What nature has not given us, we can attain through the right use of intellect. But having intellect is not enough; we need to know how to use it. What is the use of a computer if we do not know how to operate it?

This is where Aanvikshiki comes in.

Aanvikshiki is like a guiding lamp for all knowledges.
It is a solution to all problems.

—Chanakya

Chanakya explains about Aanvikshiki in the very first chapter of *Kautilya's Arthashastra*. To learn Aanvikshiki is the first requirement of a leader. Chanakya called Aanvikshiki *Prathama Vidya* and *Parama Vidya*. Prathama Vidya means 'first knowledge' and Parama Vidya means 'ultimate knowledge'. That is the importance given to Aanvikshiki. You learn to think first and then you also have to think correctly.

In our ancient education system, Aanvikshiki was taught as the first subject. It helps one to develop the intellect and make it razor-sharp. And once you have the most trained and sharpened intellect, you can be a winner. Winners need to be thinkers. Winners need to be strategists. Winners should be intelligent. And they need to know how to use their intelligence. All these abilities are developed by using Aanvikshiki. It is a logical method of analysing a situation. It is deep analysis and finding out a solution to any problem.

Aanvikshiki helps you to understand that there could be multiple problems and one solution. It also helps you understand that one problem can have multiple solutions.

Chanakya calls Aanvikshiki the guiding lamp. What is the role of a lamp? It helps us navigate in darkness. Without a lamp, we will not be able to know if we are going in the right direction.

Once your intellect starts to guide you, you will not fail. At every step, the power of intellect comes to help and guide you. This is why Aanvikshiki is called the 'guiding lamp'.

I am sure you are impressed by the term 'Aanvikshiki' and would like to know more about it. However, it is a subject in itself and takes plenty of time to understand and master this skill of thinking. For those interested, I would recommend my book *Inside Chanakya's Mind: Aanvikshiki and the Art of Thinking*[4]. The whole subject has been dealt with in detail in this book. However, for the time being, let me explain in brief what Aanvikshiki is. This will help you as a beginner.

Aanvikshiki consists of three things: Samkhya, Yoga and Lokayata. Samkhya is a philosophy in Indian knowledge traditions. It comes from the root word 'Sankhya' meaning

---

[4]Radhakrishnan Pillai, *Inside Chanakya's Mind: Aanvikshiki and the Art of Thinking,* Penguin Random House India (2017).

'numbers'. Strategic thinking needs the base of numbers. If you can think in numbers, you can easily build a strategy.

'Yoga' is a very common word today. It is associated with Yoga-asanas or the physical exercises such as stretching, breathing, etc. But 'yoga' means 'to connect'. You can connect your intellect to the higher intellect or universal intellect. It can be done through prayers or meditation. Also a practitioner of Yoga, a Yogi, is always calm and composed.

'Lokayata' means 'being worldly wise'. It is empirical wisdom required to conquer this world. If you do not know the rules of this world, you will never become a winner. So, be smart and practical using Lokayata. It is being smart and wise at the same time.

So, now think of Aanvikshiki when you add all the three elements. An intelligent person is the one who knows his numbers very well (Samkhya), who is calm, composed and connected to universal intelligence (Yoga), and also smart and worldly wise (Lokayata).

Now, just imagine a person who has such a mind and intellect. They must have mastered the art of thinking. Dive deep into the depths of his thinking and you will be amazed. You will get introduced to a whole new world.

Deep, strategic, insightful, analytical, spiritual, wise and knowledgeable, these are the words you can use to describe the person. Such a person is definitely destined to win. So, in order to become a winner in life, develop this God-given gift—the human intellect.

In order to develop this skill of strategic thinking, we will have to follow these few steps.

Chanakya's Practical Tips

What Chanakya Says

There are plenty of benefits of having a well-laid out plan. When a bridge or a dam has to be built, it does not happen overnight. There is a lot of planning and detailing that goes into it. Any successful project is like the tip of an iceberg. The actual foundation of a building remains underwater, hidden from our view, but it is very much there. Without the foundation, a building cannot stand. The higher a building, the deeper and stronger its foundation. The same thing holds true for winners too. If you want to be a winner, your planning has to be deep and detailed.

1. All of us think and plan, but most of us do that only mentally. It is all in the mind. Winners, on the other hand, have a well-written plan. Developing the habit of jotting down pointers on paper is crucial. It helps recall.

   Write things down. If it is in the mind, it can be easily forgotten. However, if you write them down, they will be permanently there for you to recall and refer to. There are many formats in which you can write down your plan. The simplest one is to have a pen and paper and jot down the points. I have even seen people take a tissue paper and write down their brilliant ideas, lest they forget them later!

   Today, you can take notes on your laptop, computer or even your mobile phone. Later, you can organize these ideas and give the plan a proper structure.

2. While planning, it is important to study a lot. Remember,

planning is not just imagining. It is not about dreaming about the future. It is a very detailed exercise. You need to study as much as possible about the activity you are going to undertake. The more you study on the subject, the better your plan will be.

Personally, I have spent a lot of time in libraries across the globe. I have studied research papers and journals on the specific projects I undertake. These studies have helped me immensely in various projects that I have undertaken. This habit helped me create winning projects. You can also take up a course on the subject you want to pursue. Not just formal courses for the sake of a degree and marks/grades, but for a proper understanding of the subject, the best practices available. Also, learn from others through case studies and practical examples.

3. This practical tip is going to be the game changer. Seek the advice of experts. Chanakya has often taken the help of experts like himself. In *Arthashastra*, it is called *Vriddha-sanyogah* meaning, 'learning from the real-life experts'. 'Vriddha' means 'elders', those who have spent their lifetime mastering a particular subject. They will show you the way to winning as they know the whole game. 'Sanyogah' means 'being in the company or association'.

So, Vriddha-sanyogah is keeping the association with experts. One needs to be surrounded by experts. Seek the companionship of experts. Be humble in front of them. Try to serve them. Be at their service. And with their grace, guidance and blessings, a new realm of insight and wisdom will be open to you.

There is a story about a businessman who was trying

his luck in a new business and, in spite of his best efforts, he was unable to succeed. One day, he was at a restaurant. The hotel manager, who was his friend, pointed towards an elderly person seated nearby, and said, 'Go and talk to him. I am confident he will be able to guide you.'

The elderly person was himself a successful businessman. He gave the new entrepreneur a few tips while sipping on a cup of coffee. Following the advice of the experienced business, he was able to turn around his business and make large profits.

4. Many a time when we make a plan, we stick to it. But the reality is that plans have to be flexible, not rigid. If you are stubborn with your plan, the danger is that you may get mentally stuck and hit a wall after a certain point. Even if an expert advises you to change your plan, you do not. It is called 'thought fixation'. The person gets so fixated with one thought that they do not want to change it. This is not a good trait to have. Winners are flexible.

Therefore, change the plan if required. The original plan can evolve. It should mature with time. The same plan may be successful in one scenario and unsuccessful in another.

Remember the winning formula: there is no one winning formula. We need to keep evolving our plan as and when needed.

Chanakya was once teaching the importance of taking a step back if required. 'Look at the arrow on a bow. It has to go back a bit to gather momentum. To go ahead, you need to go back too. It is not a setback. It is gathering strength. It is gathering momentum. If you try to attack without force, there is no point at all. So, in order to win the game, along with planning, flexibility is also required.'

It is said in *Chanakya Neeti* that the grass on the ground survives the storm because it is flexible as per the direction of the wind. The large trees break down easily as they are strong and rigid. Winners are not rigid, they are flexible. At the same time, they are focused on winning. Come what may, winning is the only thing they have on their mind. They may change the plan or strategy, but they do not change the idea of winning. This 'focus' on winning changes the whole approach.

POINTS TO REMEMBER

1. Write things down. When you write down your ideas and plans, it gives you better clarity, which leads to better strategy.
2. Study a lot. Studying in detail about the people and the situation helps you plan better.
3. Seek the advice of experts. When you do not know what to do, talk to them as they have prior experience and clearer insight.
4. Change a plan if required. You have to be flexible while working towards your goal. Sometimes a change of plan can make a lot of difference.

6

HOW TO IDENTIFY A PROBLEM AND FIND THE SOLUTION

To understand the problem, try to identify the expert who can solve the problem.

—Chanakya

We all face various types of problems in our life, some critical and some minor. However, problems are part and parcel of everyone's life. In order to find a solution to our problems, the first step would be to identify the problems correctly. If we do not identify the problem and its root cause, we will not be able to find a permanent solution to it. It is important to treat the disease and not just the symptoms.

Once, a person had gone to see a dentist about a toothache. After taking a close look at the tooth, the doctor suggested extraction as the only solution. The patient agreed to it and so as per the plan, the dentist extracted the tooth. However, after a few days, the toothache was back and the patient realized that the dentist had removed the wrong tooth! What good is a dentist who cannot even identify the tooth that is decaying?

This happens in every walk of life. In companies, there are performers, underperformers and non-performers. Many a time, performers are incorrectly identified as non-performers and removed from the job. For instance, the sales team of an organization has been working very hard to meet its target but have yet failed to make the cut. In such a scenario, the entire team might face the risk of losing their jobs. However, a closer analysis reveals that the core cause for the non-performance of the team was actually the leader of the organization. And by the time the real problem is identified, it is already too late, the organization might have collapsed.

The same is the case with political parties. It is often seen that underperformers manage to get to the top position by getting into the good books of the leaders and also by taking favours from family members and acquaintances. Such a trend gradually discourages the good and honest workers and compels them to leave the party. Thus, productive people leave the party and join a competitor, and eventually, the earlier party collapses.

In the above scenario, the real challenge was identifying the right leadership. If the people at the top are not apt for the job and are dishonest, the new leaders will also be selected in an inappropriate manner. And this trend will continue.

To get ahead in life and to deal with problems, we should develop the skill of right diagnosis. If our diagnosis is right, we can arrive at the right solution. And once we identify and are able to pinpoint what the real issue is, we can emerge a winner. In the field of management, this process of identifying the 'real problem' from its symptoms is called 'root cause analysis', which is a very logical and structured method of diagnosing any problem in hand. This is how it works. First, data is collected. Then, it is systematically organized and arranged. Experts are brought in, who collectively study the evidence and symptoms. And if required, they carry out further tests to arrive at the right solution.

Chanakya would also apply this kind of analysis. In Indian schools of philosophy, there are various methods to identify a problem. Some of these methodologies are Nyaya, Vaad-Samvaad, Aanvikshiki (which we discussed in Chapter 5), Tarka, among others.

The Chanakya Story

With his wisdom and presence of mind, Chanakya grew powerful day by day, and so did his student Chandragupta Maurya. As you rise in power, there is always the danger of revolt against the powerful. These threats can be both internal and external. Chanakya always believed that external threats are easy to handle since they are tangible, while internal threats are difficult to identify and hence challenging to tackle.

How do you deal with an internal threat that you cannot see? This is the kind of danger a person in a position of power faces. The enemy can be small or big, but if you do not identify it early on and demolish it, it might grow stronger and take over.

Being a strategic thinker, Chanakya always had a backup plan for every threat. Chandragupta Maurya was the ruler of India and under constant threat, just like any leader. He faced the threat of being attacked from the front as well as from the back. Some enemies are sly and sneaky after all! For this purpose, Chanakya planned to create an alternative palace for the emperor. This palace would serve as the backup in case the enemy attacked the main palace. Chanakya himself designed the palace. Every aspect of the building—from the raw material used to the layout of the corridors, from the flooring to the ceilings, from the personal chambers to the courtyard for secret meetings—everything was very carefully thought through. The palace also had an escape route. Chanakya, even personally, supervised the construction work, making sure there were no lapses on the part of the workers.

Chanakya grew more and more excited as the construction work neared the end, as he wanted to gift the beautiful and 'smart' palace to his king. After careful study of astronomy, a day was decided upon for the king to inaugurate the palace. A day before the official inaugural ceremony, Chanakya visited the palace and personally supervised it to ensure that everything was in order and as per his design and instructions. He went to each room and made sure things were in place. He was quite happy with the outcome. It was in fact better than what he had expected. He seemed pleased.

As he was walking out of the newly constructed palace, Chanakya suddenly noticed a few ants going in a line. It was nothing unusual, but for some reason, he carefully observed the ants for a moment. Then, he told one of the ministers, 'Let us get the king tomorrow as per our plan.'

As per the plan, Chandragupta arrived at the palace the next day. He was fascinated by the facade of the palace; it was beautiful, majestic and marvellous. He was so impressed with the outcome that he told his teacher, 'Acharya, this is more grand than my own palace. And it is so beautifully nestled in this forest, a perfect hide-out! I think I am safer here.'

Chanakya seemed pleased. 'I am honoured, my king. However, before we step into the palace, we have a task to perform.'

Chandragupta bowed down to his teacher and said, 'Your wish is my command, Acharya.'

And then taking a burning torch, Chanakya handed it over to Chandragupta. 'Burn the palace down, my lord.'

'What?' Chandragupta was shocked. 'I am not sure I heard you right.'

Before Chandragupta could ask for any clarification, the guru ordered again, 'I said, burn the palace down.'

Chandragupta had no choice but to follow his teacher's orders, though his heart was heavy. As the fire grew in intensity and the whole palace was engulfed in flames, a few soldiers, huffing and puffing, tried to make their way out of the palace. Chanakya had however locked all exits and the soldiers were consumed by the fire.

With a sense of satisfaction, Chanakya screamed, 'Traitors. They were hiding inside the palace all this while, looking for the first opportunity to strike you, my lord. I noticed a line of ants making its way inside the palace yesterday, which meant that there was some food stock somewhere. I found that to be strange. I came to the conclusion that there were soldiers hiding behind the wall from where these ants had emerged.'

Suddenly, Chanakya took a sword and gave it to Chandragupta. Pointing to the minister who had built the palace, he said, 'Behead this minister. He was the mastermind behind all this.'

Chandragupta followed his teacher's orders. Thus, Chanakya was able to get to the root of the problem through correct analysis.

Chanakya Neeti

In a process of investigation, various methods or steps are involved. One is to investigate the problem itself. The other important step is to find a subject expert who can investigate the problem for you. For instance, if your house is robbed, what would you do? Would you set out to catch hold of the criminal yourself, or would you take external help, say of the police? I would suggest taking the help of cops as they are better equipped and more experienced.

Therefore, in this context, the Chanakya Neeti that comes into play is,

To understand the problem, try to identify
the expert who can solve the problem.

Have you seen the movie *Catch Me If You Can?* This incredible film is based on the life of Frank Abagnale, who, at a very young age, successfully performed cons worth millions of dollars. The movie has a twist towards the end. The conman is offered a job in the police department! Isn't that interesting? On one hand he is a robber, but on the other, an expert. His experience as a conman would help the police catch other con artists like him. Don't get me wrong here. I am not suggesting that all criminals join the armed forces. I am trying to drive home the point that we need to seek the advice of experts when faced with a problem or crisis in life. What might be difficult for you might be a cakewalk for the expert.

Let us understand who subject matter experts, SMEs as referred to in management terms, are. They are much sought after in their respective fields, although they keep a low profile. Chanakya himself was a subject expert. In the field of strategic thinking, he was a master. He was the god of political science. Even today, after 2,400 years, we read his works to look for solutions to our problems. People perish but not their wisdom. They leave a legacy for generations to come. People turn to their works and their expertise long after they are gone.

Think of scientists who have discovered the cure to major illnesses. Modern scientists would still be referring to their findings and procedures. Every generation builds its knowledge bank on the shoulders of the previous generations.

Let me talk about my personal experience in this matter. Almost 20 years ago, when I started to explore the life and teachings of Chanakya, I found it very challenging to find a subject expert, as most considered it dead knowledge. However, I knew that Chanakya's wisdom was eternal and could not die out so easily. I decided to help myself out. I started to visit libraries, find books on Arthashastra and read up a lot of his commentaries. However, books cannot give you all the answers.

My search for a subject matter expert on Chanakya and his teachings led me to Swami Tejomayananda, Swami Advayananda, Dr Gangadharan Nair, Dr Shubhada Joshi and Dr Mangala Mirasdar. I am eternally grateful to these teachers for their guidance. I felt safe and secured under their wings. I had unwavering trust in their knowledge and experience.

If you are studying history, find a good history teacher. If you want to know about medicine, try to talk to a medical expert. Same applies to other fields as well. And with time and through the dint of hard work, one day, you too will become an expert in your line to study or work, and people will seek your advice and good counsel. It might sound a bit unbelievable now, but that's the truth. So, never give up. Never hesitate to take help from subject experts.

Chanakya's Practical Tips

What Chanakya Says

1. Never get into a panic mode when you see a problem. Problems are part of life. When faced with a problem, first try to find a solution yourself. For instance, if you have a headache, try to evaluate if it is a minor problem or a serious one. If the pain is not too acute, you can resort to taking some common medicines or try some age-old hacks. However, if the problem persists and the first aid is not providing relief, it's best to see a doctor.

   We are fortune that we are in a technology-driven era. Today, we can access information at the speed of thought. Just the click of a button or a Google search and we have access to a whole world of information. Of course, there is a flip side to it as well. At most times, the information can be fake and misleading. When at a crossroads, consult a subject matter expert.

2. At times, we are not able to solve a problem ourselves. In such scenarios, it's best to consult subject experts. For instance, if you have a serious health problem like cancer, it cannot be solved by home remedies and grandmother's hacks. You will need to see a doctor and that too without delay.

   Keep a list of subject matter experts handy. A doctor, a lawyer, an insurance agent, a financial planner, a wise and experienced relative—these are people whose help you will require from time to time. Therefore, it's best to have their contact details with you. Organizations too have HR experts, corporate lawyers, technical experts, chartered accountants and company secretaries. When emergency strikes, they are just a phone call away.

3. Now comes the most difficult part—paying the experts. Many a time, we don't know how much to pay these experts and what the form of payment should be. The best bet is to pay them as per their professional charges. Too much of bargaining is very inappropriate. An ethical professional will anyway not overcharge. Financial discussions should also be clear and upfront. There should be no confusion and ambiguity, as these can lead to confrontations and awkward situations in the future.

According to Indian tradition, you should pay an expert as per your faith and capacity. If you have faith in the person's ability, only then should you consult them and pay as per your ability. The attitude of paying also matters. It should be paid with gratitude and humility. A sense of thankfulness should be reflected in your dealings with experts.

On the other hand, some experts do not know their own value and cannot put a price tag to their advice. This is where we have to take a call. Pay the expert as per the value you find in their services and advice. If possible, give the expert a bit more than what is expected of you. The whole idea is to keep the expert happy and satisfied, so that the next time when you require their advice/service, they should be willing to support you again.

4. Keep your problems and the solutions documented. It helps for future references. This is where intelligent winners make their mark. You must have heard of the saying, 'History repeats itself'. That is true for problems as well. If you have a habit of jotting down the problems and how you cracked them, it will serve as a ready reckoner for later as well. It could be in the form of a journal or a book even! In fact, others too can benefit from your documentation and record-keeping.

Look at what we are doing here. We are referring to Chanakya's strategies, which he wrote and documented several centuries ago. Imagine, if Chanakya had not written *Arthashastra* and *Chanakya Neeti*, it would have been a great loss to humankind.

POINTS TO REMEMBER

1. Identify the problem yourself. Put some thought into it.
2. Keep a list of subject matter experts handy.
3. Pay the experts well. Do not be a miser in paying experts, pay as per your capacity and ability, and you will get the required results. The payment should be commensurate with the services they have provided.
4. Keep your troubleshooting experiences well-documented. When you keep a record of your life experiences, they can help you in the future too.

7

HOW TO EFFECTIVELY MANAGE TIME IN PROBLEM-SOLVING

He should hear (at once) every urgent matter, (and)
not put it off. An (affair) postponed becomes difficult to settle
or even impossible to settle.

—Chanakya,
Kautilya's Arthashastra, 1.19.30

When it comes to problem-solving, we should never procrastinate. We have all heard the saying, 'A stitch in time saves nine'. If we are able to solve a problem in its nascent stage, it can save us a lot of precious time, energy and resources. Putting it off will only make things worse. Therefore, the key here is to identify the problem as early as possible and then using effective time-management techniques to deal with it.

The problems that we face in our life can be broadly classified into three categories: immediate problems, short-term problems and long-term problems.

In the case of immediate problems, you may not have enough time to think, but you will have to respond immediately. For instance, if our house catches fire, we have no choice but to think on our feet. We cannot sit on it for weeks. By then, it will be too late! However, even in such dire circumstances, we should respond and not react.

Short-term problems may not be very pressing in nature. However, if we do not respond in time, the problem can snowball into something very big. For example, if we do not take care of fever at the first stage itself, the problem can become acute and sometimes even fatal. We have time in hand but action has to be taken in a time-bound manner.

Long-term problems are problems of the distant future. It may not require immediate attention at all, but it cannot be neglected either. If neglected, the long-term problem becomes a short-term problem and then an immediate problem. If we foresee a problem in the distant future, it is best to start preparing for a solution. For example, you know that you will be eventually retiring from your job. Although you might still have a good 10–20 years before your retirement, it is a wise decision to start building a retirement plan/fund. That way, by the time you retire, your finances will be in place. You will be able to handle personal obligations as well, such as your children's higher education, their marriage and your own health expenses without being dependent on anyone.

So, in order to tackle any problem, put them into a time zone. People who work on immediate problems are called firefighters. Those who work on short-term problems are like 'managers', but those who work on long-term problems are called visionaries. They are the true leaders of society. One such visionary was Chanakya.

The Chanakya Story

Like any other person, Chanakya's life too was full of problems, but he solved them in a time-bound manner. He tried to classify his problems and act accordingly. Let us look at Chanakya and learn how he solved the problems that he faced in life.

When Chanakya was a young boy, his father, Chanak, was faced with a problem. Chanak was the advisor to Dhana Nanda, the king of Magadha, which was the biggest and the most powerful kingdom in India at that point. Its capital was Pataliputra. Chanak used to advice King Dhana Nanda on matters of good governance, but instead of listening to him, the king disrespected his teacher. Finally, not able to control his anger, Chanak invoked a public awakening among the citizens.

When Dhana Nanda came to know about it, he immediately ordered his soldiers to kill Chanak. Chanak had to pay with his life for revolting against the King. After the death of his father, young Chanakya found himself in danger too. He was at a crossroads. He was furious at this atrocity meted out by the king. However, his father's friends, who were teachers, advised Chanakya to flee from Pataliputra. Chanakya knew that these elders had his best interest at heart, but he was not entirely convinced. He insisted that he stay back with his mother, who needed his support, more so since she had lost her husband. However, the elders suggested he take shelter outside of Pataliputra. He finally relented, albeit unwillingly. He learnt the importance of looking at a problem in a time-bound manner. He also learnt that to win any battle you have to be alive first. *Jaan hai toh jahan hai* (When you are alive, so is the world).

Thus, following the advice of his well-wishers, Chanakya ran away to Takshashila, where he spent several years acquiring knowledge and wisdom at the university. He learnt and mastered the science of politics. He studied all the previous *Arthashastras* written by Purva-Acharyas (ancient teachers) such as Shukracharya, Brahaspati, Ushanas, Narad, Bheema and Bheeshmacharya. With time, he himself became a scholar and expert on Arthashastra, the science of politics, and the scripture of wealth and economics. He studied warfare strategies, military tactics, good governance, laws and foreign policies, among others.

When he fled King Dhana Nanda's kingdom, Chanakya was not running away from a problem; he was preparing himself to deal with it better. So, at times, we should invest our time in acquiring knowledge and the required skills to tackle our problems. Invest in yourself, it's a long-term gain.

Chanakya was so bright that he himself became a teacher of Arthashastra at Takshashila, the world's most-renowned university in those days. But now his time had come to return to Pataliputra. His father's teacher-friends summoned him. Here, I would like to mention another important lesson: when the time comes, you should be ready to face your problems.

Chanakya could have easily forgotten all about King Dhana Nanda and the injustice he and his family had suffered at the hands of the cruel king. He could have continued to teach at Takshashila, earning accolades for himself. The truth is, when the time comes, you should be ready to commit yourself to the purpose of your life. And so did the Guru, for whom the time had come to avenge his father's death. Therefore, what was once a long-term problem had become a short-term problem.

For Chanakya, defeating Dhana Nanda was no longer a daunting challenge. He had the requisite knowledge and skills. He only needed to plan a strategic attack. At about the same time, another short-term problem surfaced—the arrival of Alexander, who was all geared up to take over India. Thus appeared two parallel short-term problems. Internally, Chanakya had to defeat Dhana Nanda, and externally, he had to send Alexander back.

The Guru had a two-fold strategy: to mobilize his own students in Pataliputra, led by Chandragupta Maurya and to unite all the kings of India against Alexander. Chanakya's strategies worked. Dhana Nanda was dethroned and Chandragupta Maurya was crowned the emperor of united India, and Alexander was defeated and sent back.

Though Chanakya was successful in his plan, he realized that, for India, to steer clear of foreign invasion and subjugation in the future, we needed noble and deserving leaders at the helm of affairs, or 'Raja Rishi', as Chanakya addressed them.

In *Kautilya's Arthashastra*, Chanakya offers long-term solution for sustainable leadership. A book that continues to offer leadership lessons even today.

Chanakya Neeti

While dealing with a problem, we have to take into consideration the time taken to solve the problem. There are various factors that come into play: the time needed to collect information, the decision-making period, the execution time and also the completion time. Chanakya has offered several tips for efficient time management in *Arthashastra*. One of them is:

He should hear (at once) every urgent matter, (and) not put it off. An (affair) postponed becomes difficult to settle or even impossible to settle.

—*Kautilya's Arthashastra*, 1.19.30

When faced with a problem, do not push it back for later. Act on it. Kabir's doha (couplet) *'Kal kare so aaj kar. Aaj kare so ab* (What you need to do tomorrow, do it today. What you need to do today, do it now)' conveys the same idea. In the current Indian judicial system, decisions are kept pending for a long time and as you know, justice delayed is justice denied. It is very frustrating for a person who is undergoing a court trial.

Winners are always quick decisions-makers. They are good at analysing situations. If required, they consult an expert and very soon they are able to arrive at logical decisions. People are afraid of taking a decision as they do not want to face the consequences. Sometimes, we take the right decision and sometimes we end up making a wrong decision. But that should not deter us from making up our mind. We cannot be indecisive all the time. We have to take a chance. We have to analyse the situation and with the information at our disposal, make a move, take a step.

A leader was once asked, 'How do you know if your decision is right or wrong?'

He said with a smile, 'I take a decision first and then make it right.'

Now, this may sound a bit arrogant or dictatorial. But that is the confidence a leader should have while taking a decision. After all, despite the analysis and fact finding, a leader has to go with his gut feeling sometimes.

In this context, the best example is that of Adi Godrej, the chairman of the Godrej group of companies.

He once said that he mentally puts problems into three categories. The first category comprises problems he can seek immediate solution to. He does not postpone such decisions. The second category of problems requires him to call someone up and take their advice. Such decisions are taken within a day itself. The third category of problems involves big decisions that have a long-term impact. In such cases, he calls a meeting with a group of people he trusts. He weighs the consequences, its pros and cons and then decides. Even in such a case, the decision could take up to three days.

At the senior level, your decisions can have far-reaching and long-term impact on the organization. So, you will have to think strategically and carefully. You may have to consult experts and then make the move accordingly.

Let us take another example of leadership, M.S. Dhoni. He is one of the most successful captains of the Indian cricket team, leading the team to World Cup victory. Dhoni is also known for his decision-making skills. Imagine the scenario: a captain has to take a decision when a billion people are closely watching him. Unnerving, isn't it? But captaincy is all about that. Leadership is all about risks, calculated risks. At times, in the field you cannot even consult your coach. You have to analyse the situation and arrive at a decision yourself. Dhoni has always kept his cool and composure even in the midst of high-pressure situations; hence the moniker 'Captain Cool'.

Another example of great leadership is Field Marshal Sam Jamshedji Manekshaw, who was the Chief of the Army Staff of the Indian Army during the Indo-Pak War of 1971, and the first Indian Army officer to be promoted to the rank of field marshal. When Prime Minister Indira Gandhi asked him to attack Pakistan, he refused. He told her that the time was not right. He chose to wait for a few months and work towards a better strategic advantage. Gandhi had deep respect for him and she agreed. And when the right moment arrived, he attacked the enemy and won the war.[5] He delivered what his prime minister wanted. These are the true leaders. Winners who inspire us.

Chanakya's Practical Tips

What Chanakya Says

1. Forecasting is a very important management skill that one needs to develop. What exactly is forecasting? It is the study of patterns and predictions regarding possible future outcomes. It is very similar to weather forecasting. In the corporate world, financial forecasting tools are available. They create sales plan accordingly. The demand and supply cycle and pattern is studied and analysed. It helps us bring a situation under control. There are various risk-management processes available as well.

   Chanakya would take 'the best-case scenario' and the 'worst-case scenario' into consideration while conducting his forecasting. You can also try such forecasting methods in your personal or professional

---

[5]Lieutenant General Eric A Vas [retd], 'The courage to say NO!' Rediff. com, 4 April 2003, https://www.rediff.com/news/2003/apr/03sam1. htm, accessed on 16 August 2021.

lives and become good time mangers.

2. Another important suggestion is to watch leaders and study their daily routines. For a leader, every minute counts. They constantly work under high-pressure situations. Yet, they are very effective and quick in taking decisions or delegating work. It is also said that, 'If you want to get work done, give it to the busiest person'. He will figure out a way to get it done.

   Leaders value their time and they value others' time too. They know that time is a very valuable resource and time gone, is time lost forever. Therefore, leaders spend their time in a very calculated and measured manner.

   Do a small exercise. For the next week, make a note of where you are spending your time. Write down everything from the moment you wake up to the moment you go to bed. Try to be as detailed as possible. After one week, try and analyse your pattern of time-spending. How much time was spent productively and how much time was wasted? You will be surprised by the amount of time you spent doing unproductive things. This could be your wake-up call. Make the best use of your time.

   Chanakya had prepared a daily time-table for a king. The details are given in *Kautilya's Arthashastra* (Book 1, chapter 19). Every minute of the king is well planned and well spent.

   To be a winner in life, you need to learn time management. Start by reading Steven R. Covey's *The 7 Habits of Highly Effective People*. It will help you structure your goals and objectives in a time-bound manner. Another worthy read is David Allen's *Getting*

Things Done.[6] It will help and guide you in organizing your life, both at the personal and professional fronts. You will be able to take better decisions. You can even join a time-management course. There are several available online too.

3. Next time you are given a project, try to analyse how much time would be required in completing it and if it is worth it. Is it rewarding enough? Not only in terms of money, but also satisfaction. Such an analysis will help you weigh your options in life.

Swami Tejomayananda of the Chinmaya Mission has been my personal guru. I have seen many of his followers requesting him to come to their office or homes. The first question he would ask is, 'How much time will it take me to reach your place?' And then he would do his backward calculation. He would plan his travel time and visit time accordingly. He never delayed taking any decision. It would be immediate and quick. If you write an email to him, you are sure to get a reply within 24 hours. He has led the worldwide Chinmaya Mission as its global leader spanning across 30 countries, with efficiency and effectiveness.

Don't take your life for granted. Although many of us believe in rebirth, we should not let this life go to waste. Make the best use of it. Chanakya valued time as well as his own life. Hence, he was such a super achiever.

---

[6]David Allen, *Getting Things Done: The Art of Stress-free Productivity*, Little, Brown Book Group; 2011th edition (2015).

POINTS TO REMEMBER

1. Learn forecasting. When we learn forecasting, we can predict the future outcomes and plan accordingly.
2. Study the daily routine of leaders. Leaders are very busy and a study of how they work on a daily basis will help you multitask every day.
3. Learn time management to be successful. Time is a limited resource, make the best of it.
4. Take time-bound decisions.

8

HOW TO CONVERT LOSS INTO OPPORTUNITY

Wealth will slip away from the foolish person,
who continuously consults the stars; for wealth is the
star of wealth; what will the stars do? Capable men will
certainly secure wealth at least after a hundred trials.

—Chanakya
Kautilya's Arthashastra, 9.4.26

Losses are part of life, but not everyone looks at them positively. In this context, let me narrate an incident. There was once a 22-year-old girl who lived with her 53-year-old father, who was nearing his retirement. His dream was to travel across the world after retirement, for which he had been saving for a long time. He had also invested in a retirement fund. While the father-daughter duo was busy making plans, her father was suddenly diagnosed with stage-four cancer. The family was shattered to hear the news. It was a bolt out of the blue. Nothing could have prepared them for this unexpected turn of events. Unfortunately, he passed away within a very short period of the illness. His daughter was not only heartbroken to lose her father so suddenly but also regretted the fact that he could not live his dream of travelling the world.

Soon, the girl started looking at job opportunities to kick-start her career. (She had already completed her graduation.) One day, as she was having a general discussion with her mother, the latter told her, 'Your father's dream is still unfulfiled. He had saved some money for his future travels. We used to talk about it. I think you should travel around the world and fulfil his dream.'

The girl understood her mother's sentiments and decided to follow her father's dream of travelling. She decided to take her mother along too, as her father would have wanted. But a fear gripped her. *What if my mother is not around when I am financially ready to travel? It may take me years to do that.*

Suddenly, an idea struck her. *Why postpone my father's dream? Why can't I travel now? If I wait for the right time, it might never come. Plus, I have not even started working. I have some free time. It will be a good change for my grieving mother as well. As Father had already saved money for travel, I might put it to good wish. After all, it was his dream to travel.*

Since she did not have enough money to travel, she asked her mother, 'Daddy had saved some money for the travel. Can I borrow from that fund? I will return it soon.'

Her mother did not understand what she had in her mind. The girl made a note of the places her father wanted to visit and the things he wanted to do there. She also did a calculation of the expenses involved and realized that she could at least start by visiting a couple of countries with her father's savings. She could even take her mother along. So, in a few weeks, both mother and daughter were off to the first leg of their dream world tour. Although nothing could take away the pain of losing a father and a husband, they felt his presence in every moment of the trip, as if they were fulfiling his dream.

Something strange happened during this time. This young girl used to take photos of the places they visited and write a travel blog. She started posting short articles on the Internet. The moment she returned home, she got a job offer from a travel company. They wanted her to write travel blogs for them. They were willing to pay her well as she wrote exceptionally well. And the best part was that she could travel at the company's expense. She was thrilled beyond words and accepted the offer.

Within a short span of time, she was able to return the money that she had borrowed from her father's savings and started sending some money home too. With her positive mindset, she was able to convert a loss into an opportunity. There is much to learn from this story.

Friends, such is life, it will throw shocks and surprises at us from time to time. But if we have a positive attitude and build a strategy around our setbacks, we can be winners. Let us look at how Chanakya converted a loss into a big opportunity in his life.

The Chanakya Story

When Chanakya's father was killed, it was a big loss for him. Given the circumstances, he had no choice but to flee Takshashila, leaving his mother behind. Years later, when he came back to Pataliputra, he was shocked to know that his mother had also passed away. The grief of losing his parents was deep. This loss only added fuel to fire and his hatred towards King Dhana Nanda was aggravated. He wanted to kill him and avenge his father's death. However, given his young age and lack of knowledge and experience at that point of time, it was an unmanageable situation.

One of the teachers, who was also the friend of his father, came to console young Chanakya. 'Vishnugupta, I can understand the grief that you are going through. What Dhana Nanda did was completely wrong. He deserves to be punished. He is not an ideal king and should be dethroned. Your loss cannot be recovered. Yet, even in such a situation, I want you to stay positive and focused. Let negativity not enter your mind. Don't let revenge be your objective in life. If you are constantly filled with rage and anger, you will become blind to everything else in life.'

Chanakya could not understand what the great teacher was advising him. However, he did not disrespect him, and the learned teacher continued.

'Son, many things in our life are not in our control. Destiny has a role to play. And we have to accept our fate and move on. Yet, if we take it in the right spirit, you will see some great blessings in that loss. An opportunity will present itself in the midst of all this adversity, but you have to keep your eyes and ears open—an opportunity to serve a greater and bigger cause.

'Your father was a great man. He cared for the citizens of Magadha. He was a great teacher of political science. And he was the advisor to the King himself. If he were an ordinary teacher, he would have been happy with the handsome salary he was getting from the king. But he decided to advice the king on his rightful duties. He stuck to his role of being a great advisor and teacher. He did not compromise on what he felt was right. He always stood for what was right and just, so much so that he even went against the King. When Dhana Nanda did not heed his counsel, he even tried to mobilize the citizens of Magadha. The citizens loved and respected your father. They agreed to support him and went against the powerful king. Your father demanded good leadership and good governance.

'Your father was not afraid to revolt against the king, against the authority. In the beginning, Dhana Nanda took the citizens' movement lightly. He thought that it is just another event that will fizzle out. He was confident that he could crush the uprising with the help of his powerful army.

'Unfortunately, your father had to pay the price for standing up against the King with his life. He may not be with us today, but his vision will live forever. Till Magadha finds its right leadership, your father's dream will remain unfulfiled.'

Then looking straight into young Chanakya's eyes, the teacher said, 'You will have to complete his unfinished work. You have to take the lead in continuing his journey forward. Wake up, Vishnu. Here is your life's biggest opportunity... to change the destiny of Magadha and India forever. Not many people get such golden opportunity. You are intelligent, qualified and also hard-working. Density has chosen you for this work. You can do it. And only *you* can do it. And in this mammoth task, we teachers are with you. Remember, God is with you.

'But do keep in mind, your vision should not be to only kill Dhana Nanda. You need to expand it from a personal agenda to a national agenda. You need to create a golden era for India. That should be your vision. If you have revenge in your mind, you will never be able to fulfil it. But if you have *Bharat Nirman,* the creation of a great nation, in your mind, you will surely fulfil it.'

Chanakya understood with clarity what he was supposed to do. And the rest is history. We are all benefitting from his vision and creation of a great India.

Chanakya Neeti

When people go through a loss or trauma, they usually get depressed. They do not know what to do, how to respond to the adversity. Our mind and intellect stop functioning, leading to a mental block. People take recourse to the easy option of blaming others for their failure, be it their fate or their destiny. Under such circumstances, they consult astrologers. They try to find answers in their stars and in astrology. Of course, a good astrologer can be your friend, philosopher and guide. In fact, an expert astrologer is also very analytical in nature. He is like a scientist and mathematician put together. In *Arthashastra,* such a person is called a Raja Purohit, the king's priest, who is also one of his key advisors.

Although Chanakya does suggest consulting an astrologer for advice once in a while, we should not undermine our own hard work and determination and become totally dependent on them. After all, we can turn our fortunes around through grit and unwavering hard work. Unfortunately, many astrologers are not qualified enough and try to mislead people. They try to make the best of people's weakness and adversities to make a few bucks. You should avoid such people.

Wealth will slip away from the foolish person,
who continuously consults the stars; for wealth is the
star of wealth; what will the stars do? Capable men will
certainly secure wealth at least after a hundred trials.

—*Kautilya's Arthashastra,* 9.4.26

Many people continuously consult astrologers. They become dependent. And that is where the problem starts. They do not put any efforts to reverse the situation at all. But not putting hard work and efforts and just waiting for destiny to make you successful is a big mistake.

Even in matters of wealth, Chanakya says that wealth will slip away from the hands of foolish people. Wealth comes to those who put in a lot of hard work. Those who do a lot of charity acquire merit and such people are truly wealthy, in the truest sense of the term.

Once you have money and you become wealthy, you acquire more wealth. It is quite paradoxical that when you are in need of money, it eludes you. But once it starts coming your way, it comes in huge quantity and starts to multiply, making you very rich. What about people who are not yet wealthy and successful?

Chanakya says that if you are capable, you will surely acquire wealth with time. Capability is the key here. Become capable. Acquire the requisite skills, knowledge and education. Try your best and experiment with the available resources. Do not give up. Even if you have to do a hundred trials, do not give up. Keep trying.

Do not fear the challenges that come your way. Learn to brave the storms that you encounter in your life. You should not stop trying. You should not bend. Take the right steps. Have faith in God and in your own capabilities. You should be convinced that you are doing great work. Take each day as God's gift to you. And when the right time comes, the tide will turn in your favour. You will reach your destination. This is nature's law. Nothing in the universe goes unnoticed. What is due to you will surely be given, sometimes it might take a little longer.

An industrious businessman was trying very hard to make it on his own, but success evaded him. He felt hopeless and dejected. He wasn't able to bear the fact that his family was suffering because of him. He was not being able to fulfil his role as a provider.

Dejected, he told his wife, 'I am sorry to see you all suffer because of me. I promise you, one day we will be rich.'

His wife smiled at him and said, 'We are already rich... we have each other. Yes, one day we will make money also.'

This is the trust we should have in ourselves. And if our family is supportive, then the struggling period becomes less of a burden and more of a learning experience. Sometimes, success can be hidden in places we never imagined. Let us look at a story here to drive home the point.

A man was running a small factory. He was ambitious and wanted to expand his business. With this purpose, he fixed meetings with several big clients, but no one trusted him enough to deliver big orders. Since his was a small enterprise, the big players in the business bullied him, leaving him hopeless and dejected.

One day, he had a visitor at his factory. He was dressed simply. He said, 'I would like to see your unit. Can you show me how you manufacture your products?'

Taken by surprise and wondering who this person was, the factory owner reluctantly took him around, explaining the production process. After the factory visit, the stranger said, 'Can you come to my office tomorrow? I would like to place a few orders with you.'

The factory owner went to meet this person the next day, unsure of what to expect. He was quite surprised to find that the stranger was a very well-known businessman. He was overjoyed to receive a big order from that group— much bigger than he had ever imagined. He finally found his dream client.

While giving the pay cheque, the successful businessman said, 'I had heard a lot about you and your capabilities but never really had the opportunity to meet you or see your factory. So, I decided to visit your unit myself. Your factory might be small, but it holds tremendous potential. You might be trying to find a toehold in the business today, but very soon, you will find yourself in a much better position. I have trust in you and, so, I have decided to place this big order with you.'

The factory owner had mixed feelings. He was excited about the big project being offered to him, but he was also anxious about being able to deliver a quality product in the stipulated timeline. As if reading his thoughts, the big businessman said, 'I know what you are thinking. Do not worry about your capacity to deliver the orders. I have faith in you. I am also ready to invest in your factory. Will you allow me to become your partner in business? It will be my privilege and an honour.'

After that, there was no looking back for the factory owner. This is how a turnaround in life happens. So, keep seeking opportunities and believe in yourself. Size does not matter. Your capability makes you what you are. Become capable and success will follow.

Chanakya's Practical Tips

What Chanakya Says

Chanakya was a strategist. A strategy is always developed through analysis. If we are able to take a step back and look at a situation in a detached manner, we will be able to evaluate it in a dispassionate way. We will be able to make an unbiased decision. We can get to know our mistakes and try not to repeat them in the future.

If a businessman has incurred a loss, it does not mean that he is a failure. He has to simply sit back and analyse the reason for the loss and then gain from that experience. This failure, this learning will serve him well in the future. If we do not fail, how will we succeed? As strange as it might sound, success and failure complement each other. It helps us understand and appreciate the other better. Failure helps us make more informed choices and take wiser decisions. Failures and losses are blessings in disguise. Let us see how to make the most of a loss or failure and turn it in our favour.

1. Analyse the kind of loss we have encountered. If it is a natural loss, we have to analyse it differently. If it is a loss caused by human error, we have to take corrective measures.

    What are natural losses and those caused by human folly? If someone dies, it is loss of life. Earthquakes, famines, floods and epidemics are all created by nature. Natural calamities lead to the loss of human lives as well as property. A society gets disintegrated. Villages and cities have to be vacated. There is casualty and those remaining in the affected areas have to relocate.

We cannot deny that such a situation seems grim. However, one way of looking at it is that destruction leads to creation. A new order replaces the old one. People learn to value their lives, and most importantly, they learn to respect and value nature. After such a widespread destruction, the financial systems and models are revised. The government relooks at its policies.

In this context, a very good example is the district of Kutch in Gujarat, which was hit by a major earthquake in 2001, killing close to 20,000 people and causing widespread destruction. The Indian government was propelled into focusing on this otherwise neglected region in a way it had never done before. Today, the district has risen from the ashes like a phoenix.[7]

Next comes losses caused by human error; for example, business losses. A deeper analysis of such misfortunes reveals financial miscalculations or the lack of a sound business strategy as the main reason. Do not lose heart under such circumstances. Learn from your mistakes and move on.

2. Many a time, instead of focusing on winning, we waste our time and energy fearing loss or failure. Our thoughts are filled with ifs and buts.

Bill Gates was once asked if the thought of failing ever crosses his mind.

His answer was: 'What if I succeed?'

Need we say more?

---

[7]To read more, Emily Buchanan and Bhasker Solanki, 'Gujarat's astonishing rise from rubble of 2001 quake', *BBC News*, 30 January 2011, https://www.bbc.com/news/world-south-asia-12309791, accessed on 27 April 2021.

3. Many a time, you may not see the result immediately. It might require a bit of follow-up. You will have to try again and again. Do not give up easily. Winners don't quit, and quitters don't win.

   'Arise, awake and stop not till the goal is reached' is a slogan popularized by Swami Vivekananda, who took inspiration in the sloka of *Katha Upanishad*. Our great forefathers and rishis knew the value of human efforts and human endeavour. They always persisted and did not accept defeat easily.

   In Sanskrit, the word for human effort is *Purushartha*. When it comes to the debate between destiny (*Prarabhda*) and human effort, it is clearly said that the latter always wins. We have been gifted with free will. Use the power of the human will and you shall surely succeed.

4. Many a time, it happens that in spite of multiple efforts, we do not win. Then we get dejected. We start considering ourselves unfortunate. In such cases, don't lose hope and faith. Just wait. Relax. Do not feel sad. Just take a step back. Probably the right time has not yet arrived. Therefore, patience is required. Allow time to pass. Patience does not mean giving up. Patience also requires effort. The ability to do your duty and patiently wait for the result is a great spiritual quality. When the time is right, you too will get your due share.

   There is another story that deserves mention here.

   A famous businessman was asked, 'How did you become so successful overnight?'

   He smiled and replied, 'Yes. I have become successful overnight, but let me tell you, it has been one long night!'

POINTS TO REMEMBER

1. Analyse your losses. It will serve as a great learning experience.
2. Focus on winning opportunities. Our focus should be on winning, not losing.
3. Be consistent in your efforts and success will follow.
4. Reconnect with the lost opportunities.

9

THE IMPORTANCE OF CONFLICT MANAGEMENT AND RESOLUTION

In a work that can be achieved with the help of
an associate, he should resort to a dual policy.

—Chanakya
Kautilya's Arthashastra, 7.1.18

It is very common to have conflicts and difference of opinion with our family, friends and colleagues. However, if we are able to manage them well, we will have a peaceful life and better relationships. In fact, not resolving a conflict is the biggest mistake a person can commit. Face the conflict or disagreement head-on and get the issue out of the way once and for all.

Conflict management is an important subject. It is used as part of organizational behaviour. There are several theories around conflict management and conflict resolutions, and many have ventured into this field as a profession. From lawyers, HR professionals, sports coaches, judges and diplomats, to ambassadors and relationship managers, all make use of conflict-management tools.

Let us take an overview of the issues that come under conflict management and conflict resolutions.

Negotiations: Negotiations are common in most conflicts. In order to be a winner and to get what you want, you need to master the art of negotiation. If the other person is a better negotiator, he will take a bigger share.

Collaborations: If you can't beat them, join them. This is a very interesting way to deal with a conflict. Instead of fighting against each other as competitors become collaborators. Think about malls where food outlets work in collaboration to attract customers. They help each other to expand the collective business rather than think about individual businesses. Together we grow!

Mediations: This is another method used in solving conflicting situations. Both parties agree to bring in their own mediator, who usually speaks on behalf of the person or the organization they are representing. They try and resolve the issue. It is advisable to have a common mediator, whom both parties respect and are willing to listen to.

Chanakya was an expert in conflict-management techniques. We discussed one of those techniques in Chapter 4. There are other models of conflict management such as the Saptanga model (seven pillars of a kingdom), the Mandala theory (circle of kings) and Shadgunya (six-fold diplomatic policy), among others.

Let us look at a story from the life of Chanakya where he looks at a conflicting situation and finds a permanent solution.

The Chanakya Story

Can a problem be solved permanently? Yes, it can be. What about enmity? Can it be ended forever? Yes, it can be. Let us look at an example which illustrates that you can defeat the enemy and still have a positive alliance.

When Alexander tried to conquer India, he failed because of Chanakya's strategies. However, there was something unique about Alexander's defeat that deserves mention here. Immediately after Alexander's defeat, Chanakya called Chandragupta Maurya and advised him to marry Helena, the daughter of the Greek general Seleucus. Chandragupta, the newly appointed king, was shocked. He was not sure if what he had heard was right.

Seleucus was a general in Alexander's army and was the mastermind behind the king's great conquests. He was also the biggest opponent and threat to India. Seleucus's strategies along with Alexander's leadership proved to be a formidable force.

Now that Alexander was defeated, he was on his way back to Greece, his country. His men were tired and homesick. They had been fighting for too long and did not want to fight any further. However, Alexander still had some fight left in him. But looking at the condition of his army, he decided to retreat. However, as they were planning to head back, he asked his general Seleucus to stay back in India.

Seleucus had a very beautiful daughter named Helena. She too was travelling with Alexander's camp. She was a great combination of beauty and brains. Being the daughter of a great army general, she was a warrior herself and had good leadership qualities.

Chanakya knew about the Greek army's strengths

and weaknesses. Although he had defeated Alexander, he respected him as a king and conqueror. He was also aware of the positives of Greek culture. Greece, like India, had many good teachers and the people held them in high esteem. Socrates, Plato and Aristotle were such teachers of philosophy. Alexander was a disciple of Aristotle. Teachers respect teachers, and Chanakya knew that Alexander was a great student of a great teacher. So, even though Alexander and his army were ambitious, they came from a great civilization and culture, and an interaction between and amalgamation of two great cultures is always enriching for both.

Seeing the look on Chandragupta's face, Chanakya began to explain the reason behind his proposition.

'In ancient Indian tradition, there were various methods of conflict management and conflict resolution. Inter-dining and inter-marriages are two of them. Whenever there is a conflict, we call the other party for a discussion and some of the best discussions happen over food. So, when there is a conflict, we have to invite the opponent(s) for talks over food and drinks.

'Next comes inter-marriages. Usually we see that marriage happens within the same community. And every community has its own practices, customs and traditions. Every community has its own strengths, which gradually develop into a subtle 'ego' hassle. The feeling of being the best and the most superior. They start looking down upon the other communities. That is when conflicts crop up. We need to respect other communities. So, when marriage brings together two communities, each grows in strength and becomes stronger.

'Marriage is a synergy between two families, two

communities. It is not just a relationship between two individuals, but rather between two families. When we respect the other person in marriage, we respect the person's community. There is much to learn from each other.

'Therefore, I am proposing you marry Helena. She will bring much experience to the table. We can learn so much about Greece and Greek culture from her. With Indian strategic thinking and Greek way of thinking, we will become a global power.'

Chandragupta was yet not entirely convinced. 'What if this plan backfires?' he asked. 'We are giving Helena the status of a queen. She will have access to all power circles. It can be dangerous. What if her father plans an attack on us through her? Also, she will be privy to all our strategic royal secrets. She might use it against us. It's a risky affair. It's like letting an enemy into your house.'

Chanakya smiled, 'You have a valid point, Chandragupta. I understand your concern. I have thought it through. Yes, the threat could be a possibility. I had studied that. But at this point, we have an advantage over them. We have been victorious in war. We are at a vantage point. The only option left for them is to retreat gracefully. I am certain they will be equally surprised at our marriage proposal, but we will win their hearts. And please note, we are not going to take Helena as a slave. We are going to give her the status of a queen. No defeated army general will ever expect that. They will consider it an honour. Indian culture teaches us to treat everyone with respect, even our foe. Since the war is over, we can become friends. This is the law of warfare, *Yudh Dharma*. Never hate your enemy. In the battlefield, defeat your enemy and after the battle, win the enemy's heart.'

Chandragupta was finally convinced and the marriage

proposal was sent to Seleucus. He and his daughter were quite pleased with the prospect. A royal wedding was organized. This marriage enabled a strong bond between the two countries. This was probably the first-ever international political marriage, which continues to be a successful model even today.

I even had an opportunity to visit Greece to deliver a lecture at the Athens University. There, I met a Greek professor, Demetrios Vassiliades. He had come to India for his PhD research at the Banaras Hindu University. His research work took the shape of a book titled *The Greeks in India: A Survey in Philosophical Understanding*.[8]

Chanakya Neeti

If you want to be a winner, understand the power of an ally. All wars will have some ally supporting you or your opponent, and your ally can also become your strategic partner. So, if you can work with the right ally, you can be a winner.

> *In a work that can be achieved with the help of*
> *an associate, he should resort to a dual policy.*
>
> —*Kautilya's Arthashastra*, 7.1.18

Who is an associate? An associate is a person you partner with to achieve certain objectives and goals. When you partner with someone, we should think win-win. As per

---

[8]Demetrios Vassiliades, *The Greeks in India: A Survey in Philosophical Understanding*, Munshiram Manoharlal Publishers (2000).

Chanakya, this is also called dual policy

Conflict-management experts talk about three scenarios when two people work on a project: win-lose, lose-win and win-win. Let us understand these three scenarios further.

Win-Lose: In this scenario, the first party is a winner and the other party is a loser. After negotiations, the first party gets all the advantages, while the second party gets minimum benefits or no benefits.

Lose-Win: The scenario gets reversed in lose-win. The first party loses and the second party gets all the advantages. In this scenario, there is a feeling of one party being a loser and the other being a winner.

Win-Win: This is the scenario where both parties are winners. Both are happy and get equal benefits. In many business partnerships, it is about having a deal of 50–50 per cent profit sharing. This is an ideal scenario.

Let us take another example of a sick company, which is not doing well financially. It has been incurring losses and the business is on the verge of shutting down. A bigger player comes into the fray and offers to take over this sick company. It is willing to buy all the shares of the loss-making company and also willing to offer a fair price. The bigger player wants to expand his business, but instead of starting his own factory, he can just start expanding through the existing loss-incurring company. He has the financial expertise to run the company and turn it around.

After due consideration, the two parties sit across the table for a formal discussion. If both parties have mutual respect, they end up in a win-win situation. The first company was on the verge of closing down. There was no hope for it at all. The second company was looking for an opportunity to expand. Therefore, it was a win-win for both.

In fact, there is a fourth scenario also. It is called win-win-win. Let us assume that the second company, after taking over the loss-incurring company, invites the owner of the first company to head the parent company. The new owner needs someone with expertise and experience to run the newly acquired company and who better than the previous owner to take over as the head. This is true win-win-win situation. The previous owner gets his finances sorted. The second company gets an opportunity for business expansion. And third, the management and its workers of the first company do not lose their jobs.

Chanakya often advised several smaller Indian kings to inculcate this model. The emperor of the country would be the supreme authority at the top level and the smaller kings continued to be the rulers of the small kingdoms. It was a good governance model under which subjects flourished.

Chanakya's Practical Tips

What Chanakya Says

1. Whenever you have a conflict with someone, it is good to voice it. Talk it out. If you keep your problems to yourself without sharing, one day you will explode, causing much hurt to others and burning bridges. However, there is a way to express your displeasure or disagreement. Respond, not react. Take a deep breath and think things over. We do not want to say hurtful things to people and regret doing so later. When you shout at someone, they

too get offended and they mirror your action and shout back. It is a vicious cycle that leads to no solution, as none of the two people/parties is listening.

So, communicating should be done in the right manner. It has to be done when the other person is in the right frame of mind to listen. If both people are willing to listen, the issue can be resolved amicably. You will also have to look at the right place, right time and right opportunity to communicate properly. Appreciate someone in public, criticize them in private. There are people who do not know when and where to criticize people. This especially happens when people are in power. There is a time and place for everything. A boss criticizing his subordinate in front of the whole team is an example of how not to resolve a conflict. The person should be called inside a room and feedback be given in private. That way, the conflict is resolved in a mature way without disrespecting the other person.

2. There are many people who are not comfortable confronting people. Either they are introvert by nature, or they are afraid to communicate effectively to others. Many are afraid of confrontations. They do not want to be misunderstood. Therefore, they can use alternative communication tools. One of the best methods is to address the problem through written communication such as an email or a letter.

Once, a consultant was called for an interview by a very big company. He was asked to quote his fees. But he was unsure if what he was quoting was right. He was asked to state the expected salary in a mail later. He wrote back a convincing mail and his stated salary was approved.

Many times in life, we have to work with people we are uncomfortable with. If we are unable to communicate our feelings properly, we should write them down.

Sardar Vallabhbhai Patel and Pandit Jawaharlal Nehru were two stalwarts of the Indian freedom movement. These two statesmen went on to become the first deputy prime minister and the first prime minister of independent India, respectively. However, they differed in their points of view and had a very different style of working. Mahatma Gandhi often mediated their differences. And since Sardar Patel and Nehru both respected Gandhi, they accepted his intervention. However, after Gandhi's death, they decided on a way to communicate with each other with least altercation. They started exchanging letters. It is a joy to read those letters between Patel and Nehru.[9]

Respect differences and communicate effectively. And also remember, differences are a strength, not a weakness.

3. The best practical tip in conflict management and resolution is to get a good mediator. A mediator does not get emotionally involved in the problem. He looks at a conflict in an unbiased way and offers the right solution. The best part is that in case you do not want to speak to your opponent, you can confide in the mediator, who will negotiate on your behalf. The mediator will understand both the viewpoints separately and come

---

[9]Section I: Selected Letters [from *Selected Works of Mahatma Gandhi: Vol. 4*], Gandhi Letter 94 : To Sardar Vallabhbhai Patel, https://www.gandhiashramsevagram.org/selected-letters-of-mahatma/gandhi-letter-to-sardar-vallabhbhai-patel.php, accessed on 16 August 2021.

up with a practical solution.

The United Nations (UN) is one such organization where all nations come together on one platform to resolve their issues. The UN plays a major role in conflict management between various nations. And due to negotiations and discussions in the UN, many conflicts have been resolved peacefully.

In the Mahabharata, Krishna was the mediator between the Pandavas and the Kauravas. He went as the 'Shanti Doot', the emissary of peace, and tried to resolve conflict between them before the Great War.

Remember, at the end of it all, we still need each other. We need to coexist.

POINTS TO REMEMBER

1. Talk it out. Whenever there is a conflict, remember, the first step is to talk it out with the other person or group.
2. Write a letter. When you cannot communicate verbally, you can write a letter to express your views and concerns.
3. Get a mediator. When you cannot resolve a conflict by yourself, get a mediator, who can speak to both parties and sort out the issues.

10

THE IMPORTANCE OF NETWORKING IN WINNING

The king, the minister, citizens, fortified city, the treasury, the army and allies, these are the seven constituents of a kingdom.

—Chanakya
Kautilya's Arthashastra, 6.1.1

There are two types of people—those who are well networked and those who are not.

What exactly is networking? Networking is the process of building relations, sharing information and keeping yourself updated about what's happening around you through others. It is a form of social interaction.

Man is a social animal. We live and work in a society. We cannot survive alone. We require each other to survive, to thrive. According to evolutionary biology, human beings have evolved due to their social behaviour of group psychology. We like to come together, stay together, celebrate together and also grow together as a species. We like to exchange ideas and information. We cannot live in isolation. If we do, we will go insane and wouldn't function at all. It is against human nature.

Therefore, the biggest punishment for human beings is to isolate them. That is how the concept of prison came into existence. Therefore, the harshest form of punishment is to isolate someone. A person who is arrested and put behind bars cannot interact with others outside prison. Their freedom to mingle is curbed. The worst criminals are put in isolation wards.

Therefore, if we want to be a winner in life, we should be able to understand the value of interacting and building relationships with others. The real winners are the ones who are highly networked.

There are several benefits of networking. But let us start with the basics of networking. Networking is not about selling a product. Many assume that by networking they will be able to sell their products and services. Networking is not just another business process. It is not just a transaction. It is about building relationships. It is about caring. It is about giving more than taking. Of course, due to networking, business too develops. It also has many financial benefits. However, if you only look at getting something out of networking, people may start avoiding you. You will not be respected, nor will you become a real winner.

So, the attitude of being a good networker starts with strengthening relationships, gathering fresh ideas, raising your profile among others and getting access to new opportunities and ideas. And most important is to get and give advice and support to others.

Chanakya was a highly networked person. We see that he knew people from different walks of life. He knew people from other kingdoms, from other places. That is what made him really successful and a winner.

The Chanakya Story

Chanakya used the power of networking to defeat Alexander. Let us know more about it.

When Alexander was at the Indian border and preparing an entry strategy, Chanakya was doing a SWOT analysis.

Alexander's core strength was the ability to inspire his army to fight and conquer the world. His weakness was that he was new to India. He had very little information about the country and its background. Chanakya realized that there was much to learn from Alexander in terms of warfare and strategic thinking. The biggest threat, according to Chanakya, was that Alexander was in a way invincible. He would try to impose his will over the citizens of India and bring them under his control, leading to a national disaster. Thus Indian culture, which has stood the test of time for thousands of years, was faced with this threat.

Next, Chanakya tried to do a SWOT analysis on himself. His biggest strengths were his knowledge and power of networking. He was a highly respected teacher of political science and was well acquainted with the other teachers of the field. Also, he had his scholar friends on his side. However, his weakness was that he was neither a king nor had an army of his own. How could he defeat the onslaught of Alexander without any weapons and ammunition? Another major drawback was that the princely kings of India were divided and involved in petty fights against each other. If they themselves were not united, how could they take on a big enemy like Alexander? Instead of taking this situation as a hurdle, Chanakya saw it as a golden opportunity to use his power of intellect and communication to bring the states together, united by a common goal. He could integrate India into one unified nation.

At that time, Magadha was the biggest and the most powerful Indian kingdom. It also had the largest army. However, despite its antiquity, Magadha lacked good leadership. King Dhana Nanda did not possess the abilities and qualities of a good leader.

After much thought, Chanakya decided to meet Dhana Nanda and seek his help in unifying the smaller kingdoms in their fight against Alexander. If Dhana Nanda had agreed to unite all the kingdoms of India against the Greek army, they would have accepted him as their leader and won the war. But unfortunately that was not to be.

What is the other solution? Chanakya thought to himself. He decided to create his own army comprising his students. He also applied his networking skills to unify the remaining kingdoms all by himself. He started training his students in the art of warfare. He appointed Chandragupta Maurya as their leader. The theoretical wisdom of Chanakya now needed to be converted into practical application.

Next, he started to influence his powerful friends. Some of his childhood friends were ministers and advisors to various kings across the country.

India at that time was divided into sixteen territorial units termed as Mahajanapadas. Since Dhana Nanda was not ready to support Chanakya, the latter made a plan to meet all the remaining fifteen kings and seek their help and support. This is where the power of networking and strategy came handy.

One by one, Chanakya approached his friends and explained his vision to them. Not many were aware of Alexander's plan of conquest. Chanakya had to convince them about the reality and the predicament that lay ahead.

Gradually, Chanakya managed to gather the support of his influential friends. They agreed to help him and arranged meetings with the remaining kings. A few of them readily agreed to support him, while others took some time to be convinced. A few did not agree to join hands with Chanakya. Thus, with the help of his students, friends and kings, he was able to put together an army comprising foot soldiers, chariots, horses and of course a large number of elephants.

When Alexander reached Indian soil, his army was petrified at the sheer size of the Indian army. Apparently, it was five times the size of their army. The Greeks had to finally withdraw. Alexander's dream of conquering the world remained unfulfiled.

This is the power of networking. One should know how to connect with the right people and use the power of influence and communication. Once the communication is perfect, and if you know how to convince others, you can win any battle in this world. Winning is also about teamwork.

Chanakya Neeti

Chanakya had understood the power of networking and seeking allies in creating a large and powerful kingdom. He also taught the same to his students. He called the allies 'mitra' (friends). No kingdom can be powerful if they do not have good networks and allies. Let us look at the importance of mitra as given in Chanakya's Saptanga model.

The king, the minister, citizens, fortified city, the treasury, the army and allies, these are the seven constituents of a kingdom.

—Chanakya
Kautilya's Arthashastra, 6.1.1

According to Chanakya, a kingdom consists of seven parts. A good king, along with a formidable team of ministers, happy citizens, a fortified city, a full treasury, a strong army and strong allies put together make a great and strong kingdom. Even if one of them is missing, there is a problem. The weak link will always destroy the whole kingdom. So, make sure you have all the seven elements in place. This will lead you to success and you will remain undefeated. You will be a winner all the time.

If you want to understand this model in detail, you can read my book *Chanakya's 7 Secrets of Leadership*,[10] which was co-authored with D. Sivanandhan, Indian Police Service (IPS) officer, who served as the Mumbai Police commissioner and Maharashtra's Director General of Police (DGP). The book offers a strategic and modern approach to building your own organization (kingdom) or business using the Saptanga model. It is very practical in approach and you can create a Saptanga plan for your personal and professional lives as well.

But for the time being, let us focus on the networking part of the Saptanga model. It is the seventh part of the kingdom—the mitra, the ally.

Swami Chinmayananda, the great spiritual teacher, used to say, 'Money never makes you rich, friends do.' We may

---

[10]Radhakrishnan Pillai and D. Sivanandhan, *Chanakya's 7 Secrets of Leadership*, Jaico Publishing House; First edition (2014).

lose all our money and wealth, but if we have friends by our side, we can win the battles of life again. They are our biggest supporters in life. That is the reason why Chanakya emphasizes the need to have friends. But also remember, we need to know who our true friends are. Some friends are genuine and some are not. We should have the ability to differentiate between them. If you network with the wrong people, it can get you into trouble. Follow the age-old adage, 'You are judged by the company you keep.'

In Indian tradition, good company is called 'sat-sangh', which also means spiritual company. The friends who are spiritual in nature will always look at your benefit. So, be careful about two things in networking. One is wrong networking and the other is over-networking. The first can get us into trouble and the second will lead to sheer wastage of time. The ones who over-network are also called visiting cards collectors. Today, many people network on various apps such as WhatsApp without an agenda. Avoid such people/groups.

So, what are the qualities of a good ally/mitra or a good network? Let us look at a few of them here.

1. **Allied for a long time:** If you have a friend you have known for a long time, the relationship is already built. No extra effort is required. You both know each other well. The more time you spend with a person, the better you understand them.

2. **Constant:** A good friend is a constant support to you. He will not be an opportunist. He will not just use and throw you. So, be constant in thick and thin. In good times and bad, your friendship should be constant. Don't be a fair-feather friend.

3. **Able to mobilize quickly:** In a crisis situation, a true friend should be able to mobilize things quickly. They should be a firefighter, a trouble-shooter. They should be your 'go-to' person.

4. **Not self-centred:** A friend should not be self-centred. Friendship is a win-win situation. It is about giving first. It is about understanding the other person before being understood. To win good friends, you need to be a good friend first.

Chanakya's Practical Tips

What Chanakya Says

Winning through networking can be done if we follow the right process. Here is how:

1. Many of us network with the wrong people. It is important to identify who the right people are. What can be right for someone else, may not be right for you. And what is right network for you, may not be the right network for someone else.

   How do you know the right people to network with? The simple tip is to do some research work about them. It starts with finding one lead. Start with one person and your circle of networking grows.

2. Once you get to know the people to network with, build relationship with a few. It is not humanly possible to know everyone who is ready to network. So, you will have to choose the right people and connect with them at a personal level.

3. One question you need to ask yourself during networking

is: what is the purpose of my networking? If you are doing it simply to while away time, then there is no point in it. If it is about gathering specific information or advice or getting a deal done, networking could really help. As they say, the real challenge is to get your contacts into contracts. If that happens, you are truly a winner.

While I was studying *Kautilya's Arthashastra*, I asked my teacher Dr Gangadharan Nair, 'Sir, is it possible for a person like Chanakya to write *Arthashastra*, which has 6,000 sutras, covering 180 topics? How can one person be an expert in so many fields?'

Dr Nair had a very unique reply for me, 'You do not have to study every subject to become an expert. Just network with the experts of each subject. They will then guide you in each of the subjects that you want to know about.'

This is networking with experts. This is a must. And the first thing to do is to give respect to every expert. They are stalwarts in their fields. They will show you the way. They know the end of the journey before you have even started it.

4. Building a relationship is not enough. You will have to keep investing in the relationship in order to make it sustainable. If you keep meeting the person regularly or call them from time to time, the relation remains strong and continuous. In many companies, there are 'relationship managers'. They are not sales people. They are assigned the task of building trust and a strong relationship with their clients/customers.

I personally know four brothers who own a big business in India. The eldest takes care of the finances, the second one takes care of the sales and marketing part. The third looks into the running of the factory and other operational matters. And the youngest is fully focused on building relations and networking. Thus, they have clearly defined roles. Someone once asked the chairman of the company, the eldest brother, the secret of their successful business. Without an iota of hesitation, he replied, 'Our winning strategy has always been networking and building relationships.'

POINTS TO REMEMBER

1. Get to know the right people. They will lead you to winning.
2. Find a way to get connected to the right people.
3. Network with a purpose.
4. Focus on winning through relationship-building.

11

HOW TO MANAGE
A WINNING TEAM

In case the employee misses the time (or completion)
or does the work in a wrong manner, he may complete
the work through another.

—Chanakya
Kautilya's Arthashastra, 3.14.10–14

To be a winner, you need to create winning teams. You might be a star performer in an individual capacity, but you might not be a good team player. You may be a winner but a bad manager. Not all winners are great team managers. Not all great team managers are great leaders. So, we will have to look at a totally different approach while creating a winning team.

As a winner, it is always about self-development, however it is more challenging to create a winning team, as you will have to bring out the best in everyone. You will have to make sure that everyone's strengths are steered in the right direction to bring out the best result. This is what makes a true leader. This is what leadership is all about. A leader has to understand the needs of their team members, and only then winning teams are created.

J.R.D. Tata was the chairman of Tata group of companies for a long period of time. When he took over the reins, the company was already established. He had to not only manage the existing companies but also take on a leadership role. Right from the day he took over as the chairman, JRD understood the importance of teamwork. He focused on creating good and strong teams, allowing the team members to shine as individuals as well. Sometimes it so happens that the powerful players in a team completely overshadow the weaker ones, stealing the spotlight. This is where the weaker players suffer, although they might have put in an equal amount of hard work and dedication. That is where a true leader steps in. He not only makes sure the entire team performs but also that each member is given due credit.

JRD was a very humble person. He was once asked in an interview, 'What has been your single biggest achievement as a leader of the Tata group?'

With a smile he replied that he had not created anything new in the Tata group. That Air India was the only new thing that he started. Everything else was already in place. He had to just manage the group through its respective company managers. He said that handling the managers of the group companies was the biggest challenge and also the biggest achievement.

He always heard them out. He always took their inputs and suggestions. Despite difference of opinion, he always respected his team members.

As the chairman of the company, he had the power to decide and take the final call in certain matters. But, most of the times, he allowed the respective people to take their decisions. And at times, he took a back foot, allowing the board members to arrive at a decision. He became a follower instead of being a leader. This is what real leadership is about—involving your team members and making them participative in every decision.

J.R.D. Tata was the longest-serving chairman of the Tata group. He was at the helm of affairs from 1938 to 1991—a good 53 years! He led the group through various ups and downs—through Independence, during nationalization and the Emergency. After all, teamwork is all about [T-]together, [E-]everyone, [A-]achieves, [M-]more.

The Chanakya Story

Chandragupta Maurya was being trained by Chanakya to lead his class. Chandragupta was young and dynamic. He was focused and also had a sharp intellect and had the qualities needed to be a strategic thinker. He was blessed with decision-making abilities. He had faith in his teachers. He was committed to the nation and was very patriotic. He also had the commitment to fulfil Chanakya's vision. He was a true leader.

However, there was one quality that Chandragupta needed to develop—teamwork. His teacher was aware of this weakness and already working towards it. He did not want to rush in such critical matters. He wanted to give enough time to his student to build his leadership skills. Patience is required to develop teamwork and Chanakya knew that.

This was the time when they were preparing for war against Alexander. Chanakya's students were driven to fight against the Greek army. The youth are dynamic and full of energy, however what they lack is direction. The biggest role of a teacher is to channelize this energy into something productive to make optimum use of the pent-up energy.

Chandragupta was a very efficient student. Given a task, he would complete it within the given deadline. It so happened that he expected the same of others too, which we know might not always be possible. That left him frustrated and disappointed. Some students are sharper and brighter than others. So, to expect the same level of competence and performance from all is unrealistic and impractical.

Just like a child runs to its mother to complain about someone, Chandragupta used to run to his teachers to complain about his classmates.

'Acharya, look at Devdutta. He never completes the given job on time. He takes a very long time. And this Parikshit, he does not even understand what task has been given to him. I have to explain a simple thing to him at least 10 times. And Umakanth makes 10 mistakes before getting it right! It's so frustrating. Acharya, it is so difficult to lead a team like this. They do not understand what I am going through. Acharya, how do you manage to handle these boys as a teacher? It must be so frustrating, right?'

Chanakya was listening to Chandragupta without interrupting. He wanted his student to vent. And finally he said with a smile, 'As a teacher, if I can manage you, I can manage them too.'

Chandragupta was shocked to get this kind of a reply from his teacher. He always assumed that he was the best student and that is why he was chosen as the leader of the group. Chanakya understood that Chandragupta was ready to learn about leading a team. He said, 'Chandragupta, every person has his own weaknesses. But I always focus on the strengths rather than the weaknesses. Yes, it is not that I am unaware of the person's weakness. Or that I am trying to hide the weakness. But if I focus too much on the weakness alone, at the end of it all, I will miss his positives and, like you, will get frustrated.

'We should try to work on our weaknesses, but that should be done in a slow and steady manner. Let me quote an example. You have leadership quality, but you are yet to learn about teamwork. It is because of your leadership quality that I appointed you the leader of the class.

'I was equally aware of your weakness, but I waited patiently for you to overcome it. I had to give you that much leverage while appointing you as leader.'

Then slowly keeping his hand on Chandragupta's shoulder, he said, 'You just complained to me about your friends. Now, can you think of their strengths as well? May be they are not that bad at all.'

That set Chandragupta thinking. After a few moments, he was smiling to himself. With a twinkle in his eyes, he said, 'So true, Acharya. They are such wonderful boys. They have several great qualities. In fact, they are better than me in several aspects. Some of them have skills that I myself don't possess.'

Chanakya was very happy that his student had just learnt the first lesson in leadership. 'Wonderful! Now that you are aware of their strengths, focus on them. Think how best to use their strengths. Also, remember one thing, in a team, there will be difference in attitude, productivity and skills, but there should not be a difference in vision. A common vision, a common goal should unite everyone in a group. Otherwise, everyone will be pulling in different directions. I am glad that all of you have a common vision of building a great nation, which is what makes you a great team. One day, when you become the emperor of India, you will require these same friends to manage the whole country. They will be your biggest assets. So, treasure them.'

Chanakya Neeti

Being a very good player is one thing, but being a good team player is a different ball game altogether. In life, we should be good players individually, but also develop the skill of being a team player. This makes us winners in life.

Now, what is the main job of a team? It is to achieve a particular goal. Without a set goal, the team will not work together. With a goal or target in place, the leader will be able to inspire everyone to reach that goal collectively. Chanakya has spoken about how if one person is unable to perform, the other team members can complete his job. He says in *Arthashastra*,

> *In case the employee misses the time (or completion) or does the work in a wrong manner, he may complete the work through another.*

—Chanakya
Kautilya's Arthashastra, 3.14.10–14

A company always performs based on teamwork. Every employee will have some drawback or the other. At times, they may fall sick, there might be some personal or family problems, they might have some function to attend or they may be going through a difficult phase in life. During such times, they may not be able to come to work. And even if they do, due to some reason or the other, their performance may not be up to the mark. Because of this, the productivity of the team might suffer. It is only natural. Such a scenario might crop up in any organization, in any field and, sometimes, even at home.

This is where teamwork comes into play. Chanakya says that in case an employee misses his target or is unable to complete a work, we should not worry. That work can be accomplished through others.

If an employee makes a mistake, we should not get into the blame game. It is very natural to make mistakes, we all do. No one is perfect. Even the most successful of people make mistakes. After committing a mistake, the right thing to do is own up and think of ways to rectify it. Trying to blame one another in a team is a colossal waste of time and also breaks the team spirit.

Let us take the example of a cricket team. There are star performers and average performers. Usually, a star batsman is expected to score a good number of runs. The stadium is packed and expectations are sky-high. All eyes are on him. Unfortunately, on that particular day, the cricketer gets out on a zero. He walks to the pavilion without scoring a run! Yes, there will be a lot of frustration. The player will be dejected. After all, the hopes of an entire nation were pinned on him.

Now, it so happens that the next batsman in line, an otherwise average performer, comes in and starts hitting fours and sixes. The crowd starts cheering for him. Soon, he hits a century and turns the match around, winning the match for the team. A negative atmosphere suddenly turns into a positive one. There is much happiness and joy around. Why did that happen?

The only reason is that 'winning' the match was more important than individual performance. This is achieving a goal through another person in the same team. This what Chanakya is trying to convey to us through the above sutra. That in case a person is unable to complete the work assigned to them, another should take over. After all, winning is the final objective for the team as a whole.

Also remember, as a game, cricket is not just about scoring centuries. It is a collective effort of bowlers and fielders as well. Every wicket counts. Every run stopped by the fielder matters. Every catch taken counts, as they say catches win matches. It is finally teamwork. This holds true for every sport.

The same rule applies to an orchestra as well. Musicians come together and play their respective parts in making the musical piece pleasant and soulful. Each of them has to play their musical instrument in sync. Even if one of them plays out of tune, the entire recital will be thrown off tune, making it sound more like a cacophony! It is the job of the music conductor to guide the group, who shows the way and ensures there is teamwork.

There is another advantage of teamwork. Individual mistakes can be covered up by the other group members. For instance, in a chorus, individually, everyone may not be a great singer but collectively, they might be able to deliver better.

Chanakya's Practical Tips

What Chanakya Says

Is it possible to become a good team player if you are already a good player yourself? Yes, it is. But for that, some effort is required. Here are a few practical tips for you to develop teamwork.

1. A group consists of various individuals. Therefore, if you want to understand your team, you will have to understand each of your team members individually. Try to study their backgrounds, individual preferences, choices, likes and dislikes, hobbies, expectations and their behaviour. You will have to make notes of all these outcomes of your study. It is like conducting a detailed research on each of them. You as a leader will then know how to make these qualities work towards achieving your objectives and goals.

2. No team can be productive without adequate training. Planning in advance and training team members is the most important job of top management.

    Your team members may be very talented, but even talented people require a little help. There is always room for improvement. For that, you will have to spend time with them, guide them, as and when needed. Nothing is more worthy an investment than the time spent by a leader in training their team. And if a leader is personally involved in the induction and training process, the team will be highly inspired. It is crucial to invest time and resources on people to get the best out of them. Big companies have huge training budgets set aside annually.

    Once a person asked a leader, 'What if you train your people and then they leave the organization?'

    With a smile, she replied, 'What if I don't train them and they stay?'

    There cannot be quality output without quality input. D. Sivanandhan, former Mumbai Police commissioner, once told me that 'training has to be of the highest order. Nothing short of world class and the world's best.'

3. One of the obstacles in building teamwork is communication. There needs to be clear and sharp communication. There shouldn't be ambiguity and confusion in the message being conveyed by the team leader. This will avoid any relationship issues, misunderstandings and internal fights among team members. Effective and regular communication can go a long way in building a winning team and also in resolving conflicts. Try and study some of the ways in which leaders communicate with their teams.

Gandhi gave very powerful and moving speeches, which united the people in India against British aggression. J.R.D. Tata is known to write letters to his team members. Some of them are documented and available in the form of books too. These letters not only inspired the members of the Tata group but also inspired many other businessmen across the globe. Amazon founder Jeff Bezos is known for writing letters to his shareholders, a habit he continues to keep. Every year, entrepreneurs Bill Gates and Warren Buffett meet their key team members, investors and shareholders and talk to them.

For leaders, feedback, reviews and meetings should be part of the regular communication mechanisms. Those who communicate are the ones who create great teams. Winning teams are created through constant communication, not just in the meeting room and board room, but off it as well.

4. Human beings have some basic needs such as food, clothing and shelter. But there are several basic

psychological needs too, and one of them is the need to feel appreciated, to be valued, both personally and professionally.

If we are not recognized at work, we feel frustrated. Sometimes that leads to a lot of negativity and it also impacts one's performance negatively. It is important to give credit to your team members to make them feel valued. Many bosses blame the team members for their failures, but try to hog the limelight. Real leaders never fall short of giving their teammates due credit. It is not only about the pay cheque after all. Even at our home, if someone appreciates the food that is prepared, the person who has cooked the meal feels content. A few words of appreciation make a huge difference.

Dr A.P.J. Abdul Kalam often shouldered the blame for a failed mission. But at the same time, if a mission that he was heading was successful, he would give the credit to his team members. Can you believe it? The humility is laudable. He had the makings of a true leader.

Chanakya would do that as well. In terms of intellect, he was second to none; he had trained Chandragupta Maurya to be a king. Yet, he himself never craved the attention and power. Instead of becoming a king himself, he continued to be a teacher, leading a simple life and working in the field of knowledge. He always gave credit to his teachers who taught him Arthashastra.

Great men are humble and work with great teams. Therefore, if you want to be a real winner, be a real team player. When you are down and out, your teammates will ensure a win for you. Success will follow.

POINTS TO REMEMBER

1. Try to get to know your team members individually to build better relationship.
2. Spend time in training and team building. A well-trained team is an asset to any leader.
3. Communicate regularly and effectively with your team to inspire them to win and stay united and motivated.
4. Appreciate your team, give them credit. Great leaders know that one has to give credit to the team, it is never a one-man show.

12

HOW NOT TO GET PROVOKED

After ascertaining the relative strength or weakness of powers, place, time, revolts in rear, losses, expenses, gains and troubles, of himself and of the enemy, the conqueror should march.

—Chanakya
Kautilya's Arthashastra, 9.1.1

In the games that we will play, there will always be competitors, opponents, challengers or rivals. Without them, there is no game at all. Where is the challenge otherwise? Where is the fun, right?

If you want to win a game, you will have to win against someone, you will have to defeat your rival. Who is a rival? Well, it can be a person or a team, depending on the game. For instance, in the game of wrestling, it is a single rival that you take on. The same is for the game of chess. In other games like cricket, hockey, football, etc., it is one team against another.

One of the most important aspects of winning a game is not to be provoked by the rivals. Many a time, the opponent will try to provoke you so that you lose your cool. Once you get aggravated, you will lose focus and concentration.

You will get distracted. Losing your focus means losing the game, and that is what they want. Also, we should not provoke our rival. It can harm us in a big way. It is like provoking a serpent.

Provoking someone or being provoked are unacceptable in any game. We should be able to play a game with a spirit of sportsmanship and healthy competition. There should be mutual respect. Both are trying to win the game and prove their worth, so hatred and jealousy should not come into play. Be a good player and give it your best shot. People should enjoy watching the game.

To ensure that there is healthy competition and fair play, a referee, umpire or judge is appointed in every game. Their job is to make sure that no provocation takes place. A player can be penalized and sometimes, even banned from playing the game for provoking. In some extreme cases, the player might be permanently disqualified from playing the game. It is called life-term ban.

Once, two players were competing against each other. They both shared the same coach. When they came to seek their teacher's blessings, he said, 'Let the best man win, but off field, both of you should forever be friends.'

The Chanakya Story

Did you know that Chanakya had a rival? No, it was not King Dhana Nanda or Alexander. Surprised? Well, Chanakya's most bitter rival was a very intelligent person. His name was Amatya Rakshas, the prime minister in Magadha kingdom. He was a highly educated and intelligent minister. He himself was an expert on Arthashastra or political science. A dynamic prime minister, nothing escaped his sharp mind.

During that time, the situation in Magadha was very poor at the leadership level. Dhana Nanda was totally engrossed in enjoying his life. He hardly spent any time in matters of governance. Drinking, gambling and womanizing were the King's favourite pass times! Even when scholars and teachers of high repute visited the kingdom of Magadha, Dhana Nanda rarely held discussions with them, thus losing out on many opportunities to gather wisdom and insight on how to rule the kingdom.

If this was the case, how is it that Magadha continued to be the strongest and the most powerful kingdom in India? How come it still had the strongest army and the treasury was always full? The reason for this was only one person—Amatya Rakshas. In reality, he was the true leader of Magadha, who was actually running the show.

Dhana Nanda was a bad king, but Amatya Rakshas was a great prime minister. He was running the kingdom through his excellent management skills. Amatya Rakshas was totally devoted and committed to Magadha. He was very patriotic and would do anything for the safety and honour of his kingdom.

In spite of all his drawbacks, Dhana Nanda had one good quality. He respected Amatya Rakshas immensely. He always used to listen to him and take his advice. He found it very difficult to say no to his minister. Such was the respect and admiration that Amatya Rakshas commanded.

Defeating the king of Magadha was not difficult, considering he took very little interest in the affairs of the kingdom. The main problem was Amatya Rakshas. So, Chanakya started focusing on defeating the king's right-hand man, Amatya Rakshas.

Chanakya laid out a trap. He sent a messenger to the

King's court to misguide Amatya Rakshas. The minister was diverted and fooled. And slowly, Chanakya sent his small army, led by Chandragupta Maurya, to defeat the king. The whole idea was to make sure Amatya Rakshas was not around when all this was happening. And Chanakya using his Sama, Dana, Danda and Bheda techniques won over his biggest rival, Amatya Rakshas.

If you want to know more about the plot and the strategy created by Chanakya, read the Sanskrit text, *Mudrarakshasa*. It is a classical Sanskrit play, written many centuries ago by the great writer Vishakadatta, which narrates the ascent of King Chandragupta Maurya to power in India.

But there is an interesting twist to the plot that Chanakya had worked out. After Dhana Nanda was dethroned, Chanakya sent a message seeking a meeting with Amatya Rakshas. When Amatya Rakshas came to know about this proposal, he was furious. However, he had immense respect for Chanakya as a teacher, and so he decided to accept the offer. When they met, Chanakya made him an interesting offer.

'Amatya Rakshas, you are a great minister. I respect you a lot. I have come here to request you to kindly continue as the prime minister of Magadha. Sir, you are a great person, you know everything that there is to know about the kingdom of Magadha. You will be a better person to guide Chandragupta than me.

'Magadha needs a new leader. Chandragupta is very efficient, I have trained him well, but he requires your guidance and experience. Who better to guide him in the affairs than you? Remember, it is not about Dhana Nanda or Chandragupta. It is about our great Magadha kingdom. It needs a leader like you.'

Finally, Amatya Rakshas was convinced that Chanakya only had Magadha's best interests at heart and willingly accepted the offer. This is mutual respect. Respecting one's rival and making him part of your team takes a lot of courage and humility. Not everyone can do it.

Chanakya Neeti

If you want to be a winner, you need to be a strategist. And strategy begins with studying one's competition. You need to plan in order to win. Only dreaming about winning will get you nowhere.

After ascertaining the relative strength or weakness of powers, place, time, revolts in rear, losses, expenses, gains and troubles, of himself and of the enemy, the conqueror should march.

—Chanakya
Kautilya's Arthashastra, 9.1.1

Before you attack, plan your attack. Look at the various dimensions. We need to look at the enemy's relative strengths and weaknesses. We had previously read about SWOT analysis.

The same rules apply here. We need to understand the enemy completely.

Nowadays, it is common practice to closely watch a few previous games played by the competitor. This gives a good overview of the opponent's strengths and weaknesses. You can then plan your strategy around those. This is where 'opportunity' lies.

Winning is also about being at the right place at the

right time. A product that sells very well in one place might not sell in another. You might be pitching a very good idea to your team, but since the time is not right, it may fall on deaf ears.

For instance, in India, most movies are released during the festival and holiday time. People are in a celebratory mood and spirits are high. In other words, it is the best time to cash in. So, it is all about timing. Also, we need to respect the place. Today, people do not just go to movie theatres, they also watch movies online. Your mobile device gives you the opportunity to choose your own time and place for viewing. Online platforms such as Amazon, Netflix, hotstar and others have given us immense flexibility to choose our own time and place to watch movies and series.

Also, we need to prepare ourselves for the kind of competition we might face in future. Let's look at an example. An FMCG company was preparing to launch a new product. The announcement was made and the marketing strategy was in place. Suddenly, on the day of the launch, the marketing manager did not turn up for the event. It was later found that he was offered a job by a competitor and he took it. Luckily, the CEO took charge on the launch day. The product was an overnight success.

In order to develop a foolproof winning strategy, we also need to do a lot of calculations such as losses, expenses, profits and gains. This way, we know how much money we can put into the whole project. A good financial acumen gives us a competitive advantage over our competitors.

Let us take an example. Two companies were working on a similar project. Over a period of three years, one company became very profitable, while the other company was on the verge of closing down. The company owners met. The owner of the successful company was asked by his competitor, 'How come you are so successful and I am losing the game?'

The winner said, 'You focused on product development, while I focused on financial development. That made the difference.'

It is not that you should not focus on product development at all. But without a financial plan in place, even a well-developed product may fail.

No game is ever played without the possibility of losing, without the possibility of getting hurt. No pain, no gain. Nothing in life comes easy. If you want to play sports, be ready to get injured and lose. You should hope for the best but, at the same time, prepare for the worst. That holds true for sports as well as for life in general.

Always have a mentor and advisor by your side. They will guide you during the troubled times and show you how to overcome them. It could be a family member, a friend or a professional advisor. Sometimes, when we find ourselves at a crossroads and find it difficult to make up our mind, we should talk to someone we trust, someone who knows us well. Sometimes, a third person's perspective really helps.

Chanakya's Practical Tips

What Chanakya Says

It is natural to get provoked. Many a time, the rival will use this as a tactic against you. They know that if you lose your patience and get provoked, you will react. And that will act in their favour. Their main purpose is to make you 'reactive' and your strategy should be to give a 'response'.

What is the difference between reaction and response?

Reaction is an emotional outburst and not necessarily thought through. While a response is about taking a decision with proper thought. A reaction is usually spontaneous, whereas a response is planned and deliberate.

Follow these tips and you will learn how to respond rather than react to a situation.

1. Winners have a lot of patience. It is not that they do not have problems, but they have developed patience as a virtue. They know that the golden rule in life is 'I may be slow, but I am sure'.

   Remember, when someone provokes you, you have a choice—either to get angry or develop patience. Anger is a punishment you inflict on yourself. And if you punish yourself, the rival is going to benefit from it.

   Also, if you get angry, you are giving your power to someone else. Think about it like this—you have a thousand rupees with you. And if someone asks for it, either you give it or you don't. So, if you have power with you, why will you want to give it to someone else? By provoking you, they snatch away your power.

2. Being cool is a great thing! When you are provoked, at least try to say cool. Your competitors will be looking for an opportunity to distract you. They will be studying your body language. Don't give in.

   The best way to deal with provocation is to take a deep, long breath. Once you practise deep breathing, your mind calms down. You regain your composure. You will be able to think straight. There is a deep connection between the body, mind and soul. All three must be in sync. The slower and steadier your breathing, the calmer you are.

Another method to deal with provocation is to mentally count till ten. It is a tried-and-tested method.

You will be surprised how your mind calms down. You must be wondering about the logic behind this. When a person reacts while being provoked, the reaction actually happens in the first five seconds. After those five seconds, you start thinking logically rather than emotionally. Therefore, when you count till ten, somehow you have crossed those crucial five seconds. Your mind then starts to analyse the situation logically and you make smarter decisions.

3. When you are provoked, think of your rival as a child. Visualize him as a little child throwing tantrums. Now, invoke the adult in you. Your inner adult will look at that situation from a matured standpoint. Think of yourself as a parent or, even better, as a grandparent. They know that the child is only reacting. They are fully aware that it is a temporary phase and will soon vanish.

   In fact, when a rival provokes you, try to enjoy the moment. They will be surprised that instead of reacting, you are actually enjoying it. Indirectly, you will be provoking *them*. They may react instead. And that gives you an advantage over them. This is another way of winning over a rival.

4. Imagine yourself in a situation where someone is trying to provoke you. It can be your boss in office. Or it can be your class teacher. If they shout at you in front of others, you react and shout back at them. Now, visualize the scene, what would happen after you shout at them? The reaction can lead to a different situation. You can lose your job. You might be thrown out of the class. Such reactions have a ripple effect. In case you are in

a sports team and you react to a provocation, you may lose your place in the national team, which you have achieved after years of hard work.

When faced with a situation where someone is trying to provoke you and you want to react, think of the consequences. Is it worth it? Will your reacting backfire? So, friends, the summary is that to be a winner, you need to stop reacting and start responding more.

When King Dhana Nanda killed Chanakya's father, he could have reacted and tried to avenge his father's death. But young Chanakya didn't stand a chance against the mighty king. He too would have been killed. Therefore, he responded by facing his arch-rival, the king who took his father's life, only when he was better equipped to win.

POINTS TO REMEMBER

1. Develop patience. Winners know that patience is a virtue to be developed through practice.
2. Be cool. Being cool-headed helps you handle every situation with a strategic mindset.
3. Invoke your inner adult. It will help you deal with a situation better.
4. Don't make a fool of yourself by reacting to people and situations. Even if you don't know what to do in a given situation, at least try to pretend that you are not provoked.

13

HOW TO MOTIVATE YOUR TEAM IN DIRE NEEDS

Give up a member to save the family,
Give up the family to save a village,
Give up a village for the country,
And give up the world to save your soul.

—*Chanakya Neeti*, 10.22

D. Sivanandhan got a call from his senior informing him that he was being transferred to Mumbai on an urgent basis. He had been promoted as Joint Commissioner of Crime. This was great news. It was an important position which came with its share of responsibilities. But with great power comes great responsibilities. Being in charge of law and order in Mumbai, the hotbed of the underworld, was a big responsibility. The police was constantly in a tussle with the mafia. Crime rate had gone up like never before. The financial capital of India was under tremendous stress. There was deep-seated fear in the minds of the people.

The police department knew that if there is one person who could perform under this kind of stress, it was Sivanandhan. When he took charge of Mumbai Police, the first thing Sivanandhan did was to motivate his team. This is where leadership plays a major role. If the team is not motivated, the leader cannot accomplish the task alone. And that is exactly what Sivanandhan did.

When Sivanandhan finally got into attack mode, over 300 gangsters were killed (neutralized) and over 1,000 put behind bars. A new law was created named MCOCA (Maharashtra Control of Organised Crime Act, 1999). Gangsters were now afraid of the law. This helped the police regain the confidence of the people, without which they would be demoralized. Note that the Mumbai Police team was the same as earlier, it was only the leadership that had changed. The approach of the leader made a big difference. With the help of the police, the business community, too, was assured of their safety. Today, Mumbai is considered one of the safest cities in the country.

If you want to know more about the strategies applied to pull up the team and achieve the goals by Sivanandhan, read *Chanakya's 7 Secrets of Leadership*.

Many people think that one person cannot make a difference, but the truth is that one person can make *all* the difference. Great leaders can make or mar a nation. Never underestimate the power of one person. Chanakya was one such leader and motivator.

The Chanakya Story

To motivate employees may be easy as they are getting paid for their job, but to motivate young students is a challenge because of two major reasons. First, students, being of that age, are unable to understand the difference between right and wrong. They can be easily misguided too. The second reason is that students are still under the influence of their parents. The most important decisions are taken by the parents on their children's behalf.

Chanakya was trying to put together an army of young boys to fight against Alexander and also dethrone King Dhana Nanda of Magadha. A solider is always at risk of losing his life in battle. Hence, the students' parents were unwilling to send their young sons to war. No family would want to lose their young children in battle. So, Chanakya was faced with the challenge of motivating not only his students but also their families. He devised a plan to tackle the situation.

First, he made a list of students who were getting pressurized by their parents and family members to leave Chanakya's gurukul. Second, he decided to personally visit the family of every single student.

When Chanakya visited the first student's house, the student was very excited to see him. He ran out of the house to greet his teacher. As soon as the student bent down to touch Chanakya's feet, his mother came from inside the house and pulled him back.

'Go inside, son. I order you. This man who calls himself your teacher has come to snatch you away from me.'

With his head lowered, the student started walking towards the house slowly.

Chanakya knew how to convince his mother. He simply stood at the threshold for a few seconds. The mother expected Chanakya to walk away, but he did not. After sometime, he asked her, 'Can I get some water? I am thirsty and hungry too.'

The mother could not say no. She knew that, after all, he was her son's teacher. Immediately, she invited him inside and offered Chanakya food and water. This was the opportunity Chanakya was looking for.

He asked her, 'How will you feel if someone attacks you physically and your son keeps watching everything from a distance?'

The mother was taken aback by this question.

'Will you not feel bad that your son is being irresponsible and worthless?'

She nodded her head but could not say anything.

'This is the sad part, that you, as a mother, do not understand the value of our motherland. Because he has taken birth from your womb, you consider him your son. But you do not understand that this great motherland of ours feeds us, nourishes us and takes care of us every day, just like a mother. What we are today is because of her. And now that someone is going to attack her, you want your son to just wait and watch? I cannot accept this food and water from someone who does not love and respect their motherland,' saying this, Chanakya stormed out of the house.

The mother ran behind him, requesting him to come back. 'Acharya, please forgive me. I see your point and agree that we were being selfish in trying to hold back our son from fighting for the country. We happily grant permission. Please take him along with you to the gurukul.'

Chanakya smiled at her and as if revealing a plot in his head, said, 'Even if you had not given permission, I could have easily taken him away, but I did not want to do that. I want you to be with us in this. He needs your blessings.'

This is how slowly but steadily Chanakya managed to convince the parents to allow their sons to fight the war against Alexander.

Chanakya Neeti

We should never be selfish and only think about ourselves. Leaders make sure that they show their team a higher purpose in their lives. That the work they are doing is not ordinary, but something very different and big. They show them a vision.

> *Give up a member to save the family,*
> *Give up the family to save a village,*
> *Give up a village for the country,*
> *And give up the world to save your soul.*

—Chanakya

Let us try and understand what is being said in the above quote.

Family: In every family, there will be difference of opinion and fights. However, if a member becomes an absolute nuisance and poses a threat to the unity and well-being of the family, they should be corrected at the right time.

Village: Some families have to make sacrifices for the sake of the village. For example, the development of a village is being planned through the construction of a road and your property comes in the way. In such a case, you should sacrifice your land for a bigger cause; in this case, the welfare and development of the village.

Country: When a country is making progress, new infrastructure has to be created, such as dams, bridges and roads. Under such a scenario, villages sometimes get uprooted. This is a sacrifice that a village makes for the overall development of the country. Sometimes, an entire village might have to fight an enemy who has attacked the country. This is another form of sacrifice.

World: Sometimes we might have to renounce all our worldly possessions for spiritual advancement. We should not consider this a loss or tragedy. Many rishis and learned men have sacrificed their earthly possessions seeking knowledge and enlightenment. Such people are truly blessed as they have found the Light.

These are some of the scenarios where people get inspired to fulfil a certain vision. So, if you want to motivate your team, you will have to show them a higher purpose. Generally, people do not like to give up what they have. Therefore, they need to be shown that what they will have later is all worth it. Otherwise, we will be penny wise, pound foolish. The leader's job is to ensure that the higher purpose is achieved. That is real motivation.

Einstein had said, 'We cannot solve our problems with the same level of thinking that created them.'

A child will not leave his school friends unless he understands the value of going for higher education at a college or a university.

When Lal Bahadur Shastri was the prime minster of India, the country was going through a rough phase. Right from the Indo–Pak War of 1965 to an acute food shortage, it was a difficult time for the country.

He gave a clarion call: '*Jai Jawaan, Jai Kisaan* (Victory to soldiers, victory to farmers)'. He knew that at both levels, the country needed inspiration. At that point, both farmers and soldiers needed a vision. Under the able leadership of Shastriji, the country was able to face one of the most turbulent times post-Independence. He focussed on strengthening research in agriculture. He helped set up the Indian Council of Agriculture and laid the foundations for the Green Revolution. He also requested the people to skip one meal a day at least once in a week. People listened to his advice. Even hotels and restaurants were shut. The entire nation was united. Everyone was doing their share to be a part of the vision. That is real inspiration!

There is another story that is worth a mention here. A man was travelling along the road when he saw a few people breaking stones. He stopped and asked them what they were doing.

The first man said, 'As you can see, I am breaking stones. This is my job.'

He moved to another man. The second man said, 'I am earning bread for my family.'

Then, he moved to the third person, who said, 'There is a temple being built here. And I am breaking stones that are to be used in the construction work. Many people will be benefitted from the temple. I am doing my bit. This is how I am contributing to that vision.'

The work assigned to all three people was the same— they were breaking stones. But the vision was different for each one of them. While the first person just looked at it as a task that had to be completed, the second man considered it a way to earn a living for his family. For the third man, he was doing his share to be part of a larger picture, a vision.

Change your vision and your attitude changes. No work is big or small. It is the vision that matters. Leaders need to understand this part.

What Chanakya Says

One should know how to communicate our vision to others. This is what you should do.

1. Communication is much needed. A leader's first duty is to clarify and communicate the vision or the purpose they are together for. The team needs to know where they are headed.

   In war, it's called mission. The leader usually picks his team members. Next, he gives them clarity about the mission and the operations they will be taking up. If his teammates have any doubts or questions, it is his duty to clarify those. Once you are on a mission, there's no looking back. It's do or die.

   Remember the scene in the movie *Uri: The Surgical Strike*, where the team leader instills a deep sense of confidence in his team. And the war cry is the leitmotif of the film—'How's the josh?' to which the reply is 'High, sir'.

2. A team leader's role is to ensure that the participation of each team member is 100 per cent. It should not be that ten people are doing the work of twenty. Each and every member should be equally involved in some way or the other. This is where delegation comes in. The team leader should access the strengths and weaknesses of the teammates and assign work accordingly, even if it is a small role. Everyone should be a player. Even if one person is left out, they will feel negative about the whole situation. So, engage one and all in the process. It is also called optimum utilization.

   I had once attended a school's annual day

celebrations. After the event, the principal came up to me and said, 'We make sure *all* the children participate in the function.' There were about 5,000 children in her school, but everyone got a chance to perform. Her rationale was that every parent who comes to see the annual day function would eagerly await their son's or daughter's performance. Hence, her priority was to get every student involved. I found her effort commendable.

Coach everyone in the team. Be kind to your team members. It is important to be a person who ensures discipline, but being kind and empathetic is equally important. Take care of your people. Give them a good and clean environment to work in. Ensure good hygiene. Your workplace should be inspiring and motivating.

Fill up the place with motivational quotes and inspiring messages. Create inspiring workplaces. Pay your people well. Take care of them and they will take care of your work.

3. You as a leader cannot do everything. You have to assign work, but let them do it on their own. For that to happen, it should be ensured that they are working as a team even if you are not around. Learn to delegate work. Let them plan and give them the freedom to experiment.

Tell them what to do and how to do it and then leave it to them. It is important that they learn to manage the work through collaborations. Encourage them to interact more and exchange ideas among themselves. A good team is the one that communicates regularly.

I was once invited to a company where we were conducting a programme called 'C2C' (meaning 'Connect to Connect'). It was a big multinational company with multiple projects running simultaneously. Thousands of employees were working in over a hundred different projects. Most of them did not even know what the others were doing.

The objective of the two-day meeting was to help the employees get to know each other better and also the projects the others were working on. A lot of ideas were exchanged. There were brainstorming sessions. The meet was a huge success. The team-building exercise was a hit. The result? The company registered a profit that year.

4. Let us not forget to celebrate together. Yes, teamwork is not just about working on certain projects or missions. It is also encouraging happiness. It is also a celebration of being together. When people work in teams, they become like families.

J.R.D. Tata was once asked if he wanted India to be an economic superpower.

'I want India to be a happy country' was his reply.

POINTS TO REMEMBER

1. Clarify and communicate your vision to your team. If the vision is clearly communicated to others, they all get inspired to work towards it.
2. Get everyone engaged in the work. Do not leave anyone behind.

3. Encourage collaboration. Instead of competition within the team, encourage collaboration.
4. Encourage happiness.
5. The team should look at happiness quotient as an important part of the process.

14

HOW TO CONTROL YOUR ANGER AND HARNESS IT

Nothing more than passion causes distraction,
No bigger enemy than delusions of the mind;
Nothing burns more than anger,
No bigger happiness than an enlightened mind.

—*Chanakya Neeti,* 2.12

Anger is one of the most basic emotions. It is an emotion that we all feel. It is very natural to lose your temper. Sometimes people and certain circumstances or situations make us angry. It is okay to feel angry, but we should have some amount of control over our temper. We should not let our temper get the better of us. Sometimes when we are infuriated, we end up saying or doing things that we might regret later. So, when angry, take a deep breath and let that moment pass.

One of the hottest topics discussed in self-help books and life-management skills classes is how to control one's anger. Anger management is an important area of study and research, and many people specialize in it too.

So, the first and the most important question here is:

is it possible to control anger? The answer is yes. All of us must have gone through such moments, when we were able to control our anger. Try to recollect those moments. You were angry and wanted to react/retaliate, but due to some reason, you had to hold yourself back. You were perhaps angry at your class teacher, school principal, a policeman, a senior family member or boss. We had no choice but to swallow our anger. In such a situation, we had to control our anger out of compulsion.

Again, we were perhaps angry at someone or something, but we controlled our temper out of choice. You might have been in a superior power and position, yet you chose to control yourself. It could have been with regard to a subordinate, a younger sibling or your employee. They must have done something that angered you, yet you controlled yourself. This is when we control our anger out of choice.

In the first case, you did not have a choice as you were powerless. In the second situation, however, you had the power, yet you controlled your temper. The second situation is worth studying here. When you controlled your temper by choice, how did it feel? Were you proud of yourself? Did you feel like you had done the right thing?

Anger is a punishment that we inflict on ourselves for someone else's mistake. There is a famous saying: 'Control your anger, it is only one letter away from danger'. So true! If we cannot control our anger, it can lead us to a dangerous situation.

The first step in this direction is self-control. Chanakya says that an ideal king is the one who is crafted out of self-discipline and self-control.

In the chapter on 'Training of a King' (Book 1 of *Kautilya's Arthashastra*), Chanakya says that a true leader is *Indriya-jaya* ('Indriya' means 'sense organs' and 'Jaya' means 'victorious', so literally translated as 'conqueror of senses'). Therefore, in the Indian Puranas, the king of gods is also called Indra.

The Chanakya Story

Is anger a negative feeling? No, not at all. We need to harness the energy that comes out of being angry. Direct the surge of emotions towards something constructive. When we do not direct it, it becomes a problem. If you can channelize the energy, it can be utilized for something good and productive.

Anger is like dam water. If you build a dam around the flowing river, you create a reservoir of energy, which is used to generate electricity. Chanakya knew exactly how to do that. He knew how to give direction to anger and how to turn it into something productive.

Once, Emperor Chandragupta Maurya asked his guru, 'Acharya, I want to ask you something important. A doubt has been lingering in my mind for a long time. I have been deeply concerned and wanted to discuss the same with you. Can I seek your permission to ask you the question?'

Raj-Guru Chanakya replied, 'Go ahead, speak your mind. I will answer all your questions. Leaders should have clarity on everything they do. Ruling a kingdom with confusion leads to utter chaos.'

'Acharya, you are aware of the various problems in Magadha. You have been in Pataliputra for so many years. And your days in Pataliputra have not been rosy.

'You were witness to your father being killed by the king. You had to flee to Takshashila and when you returned, you learnt that your mother was no more. So much pain

Dhana Nanda has inflicted on you!

'When Dhana Nanda was defeated, you had the power to kill him. His life was at your mercy. Why did you send him back alive? You just let him go into a forest and retire from the activities of the kingdom. Ever since I became the king, I have been wondering why you let him off so easy. Is it not dangerous? He can always come back and attack you. Is it not you who taught us to never to trust an enemy? Please explain why you acted the way you did. This answer would be my biggest lesson in Raj-Neeti. Your answer will resolve my inner conflicts.'

Chanakya gave a warm smile, 'This is a brilliant question, my dear Chandragupta. I am glad you finally raised it. I know it has been lingering in your mind for a while now. The first and the most important thing a person should know is how to control one's anger. Anger is the most dangerous thing in the world and when directed towards the enemy, it can prove to be disastrous.

'I too was young like you and wanted to avenge my father's death. But my teachers guided me. They told me that if I do not channelize my anger to a better and bigger vision, I cannot achieve anything in life. It took me some time to understand what they were saying. But today, I understand what my teachers told me was right. My aim was not just to kill Dhana Nanda but to make India safe and secure. When you became the king, my mission was complete. Why should I continue to direct my energies towards Dhana Nanda? He was a problem that has been solved.

'And as far as Dhana Nanda's coming back to attack me is concerned, that is impossible. I have sent him to the forest to spend the rest of his life in contemplation and meditation. Let him reflect on his own faults. Maybe he will have a better afterlife. And if at all he decides to plan a comeback attack, I am always ready. But that will not happen. My people are constantly observing his every move. They keep me informed.'

Chanakya Neeti

Chanakya did not only stress anger management but also practised it. He not only trained kings to control anger, but made sure that even common man is educated about anger management.

> *Nothing more than passion causes distraction,*
> *No bigger enemy than delusions of the mind;*
> *Nothing burns more than anger,*
> *No bigger happiness than an enlightened mind.*

> —*Chanakya Neeti*, 2.12

Let us look at the above quote in detail.

Passion causes distraction: A person who wants to be successful in life should avoid any type of distraction and the biggest distraction is passion or lust. Passion is negative energy. The desire becomes a possession and then our minds will never be at rest.

One of the biggest hurdles in achieving something is lack of concentration. Concentration is an important component in Swami Vivekananda's *My Idea of Education*.[11] He said that all energies get focused through the power of concentration.

---

[11]Swami Vivekananda, *My Idea of Education*, Advaita Ashrama, 2010.

As a generation, our biggest problem today is lack of concentration and focus. Attention span has reduced like never before. With cell phones and social media, we are unable to focus on anything for more than a few seconds. We need focus and concentration to be successful. These are the skills that we all need to work on.

Delusions of the mind is the big enemy: The mind is a double-edged sword. It can create and it can destroy. It has the power to imagine, but the same mind can imagine wrong things and create delusions. They are not real or logical. They are not reasonable. They are just mental creations. And if created wrongly, they can be the most dangerous self-destructing tool. Delusions give you a very skewed picture of the reality.

Anger burns the most: Fire burns everything that comes in its way. Similarly, anger burns from within and everything we have created outside is destroyed by the anger we have raging inside. It is like a slow fire that keeps growing bigger and bigger. It can consume a person. It can break relationships. When we are angry, we say hurtful things and get aggressive. This can lead to broken relationships and shattered homes.

Real happiness: What is real happiness? The truly happy person is the one who has an enlightened mind. Moksha should be our main aim in life. Nirvana is another word for it. Even kings and emperors in India were told to give up worldly pleasures and powers in search of enlightenment. It is not easy to renounce worldly possessions to embark on a spiritual journey. The most powerful person is the one who has reached the ultimate pinnacle of enlightenment.

Gautama Buddha, Mahavira, Rama, Krishna and Guru Nanak were such enlightened souls.

What is the use of enlightenment? Till you set out on a spiritual journey, you will never understand its value. Most people are content with the little joys of life. There is nothing wrong in that. But remember, those are not permanent in nature. These moments are transient. We keep searching for happiness outside us when in reality, we will find it within. So, make that inward journey. Introspect.

This is the story of a Zen master. He had a warrior student. Before going to war, the student took his master's blessings. 'Sir, we might be imprisoned in war?' he asked.

'Getting imprisoned is fine, but do not get into the prison of the mind. Be free always.'

It so happened that the warrior was taken captive. He was put in prison. Every day he would look out of the window and watch the beautiful sunrise and sunset, enjoy the chirping of the birds and look at the trees and flowers outside. He started meditating inside the prison. Finally, he got so involved in his spiritual practices that he attained enlightenment. His mind was free. All the inner bondages were released. He had attained ultimate happiness.

Very soon, sitting inside the prison, he started making an escape plan. When the time came to escape, he was ready. Free from his enemy's clutches, he came back to the Zen master and thanked him for the direction given.

The Zen master asked him with a smile, 'So what lesson did you learn?'

The warrior said, 'I need to conquer my inner enemy first before conquering the outer enemy.'

This is the ultimate war strategy. Anger is one's worst enemy. Once we conquer anger, we can conquer the world.

Chanakya's Practical Tips

What Chanakya Says

Before we get into the practical ways of managing anger, let us take a quick look at the definition of anger. Anger is a strong feeling of annoyance, displeasure or hostility. So, first things first, anger is a feeling. It is an emotion. It is a thought. So, to manage anger, you need to manage your feelings, emotions and thoughts. Strong people learn to control their feelings, emotions and thoughts. This is the self-control or control over the mind.

If you practise the following points, you will be in better control of yourself:

1. Meditate. This is the first step to anger management. Meditation is about watching your mind and its flow of thoughts. Many beginners get frustrated because they cannot bring their mind to a standstill. They get distracted easily.

   This is a fundamental mistake. You cannot stop the mind and its flow of thoughts in the initial stages. It is a slow process. It takes time. It takes immense practice. Zen and Daoist meditators attempt to reach the state of Mushin (in Japanese) and Wuxin (in Chinese), translated as 'no mind'.

   Years of slow and steady practice leads us to the ultimate state of meditation called *Chitta Vritti Nirodhah* ('Chitta' means 'mind/consciousness', 'Vritti' means 'waves, fluctuations' and 'Nirodhah' means 'to control, to quieten'). It is a state of mind where there are no thoughts. Practise meditation every day with deep breathing techniques and slowly you will progress. Even if you are able to sit quietly for 15 minutes at one place, it is a good start.

Same goes with anger. In the initial stages, it is not possible to control anger totally. But slowly and steadily we will get there. Do a small exercise. Make a note of the number of times you lose your temper on a daily basis. Next week, go back to the journal and read when and why you got angry. Try to evaluate if it was avoidable. Try to think of other ways in which you could have handled the situation. This exercise will help you bring down your level of anger as you introspect.

2. Read spiritual books. There is a lot of literature available both online and offline. Start with whatever interests you. It could be any spiritual book of your choice—The Bhagavad Gita, the Upanishads, the Ramayana, the Mahabharata, the Bible, the Quran, Guru Granth Sahib and Agamas.

It also could be life stories and biographies of great men and women, of saints and sages, and about their teachings. You choose. But read a few passages every day. That will help you develop a good habit of reading about spirituality. There is a difference between reading books and reading 'good books'. Good books inspire you and take you to a higher level. They help you evolve. They elevate you. These books are replete with life lessons and worthy advice.

3. What kind of a friend circle do you have? Do you have friends who are angry by nature? Are they involved in passion-driven activities such as drinking, gambling, gallivanting? If this is the case,

then slowly their nature will rub off on you too. So, it is important to choose your friends wisely. If required, change your friend circle. Be aware. Be alert. Wise people and wise friends change your life positively forever. They help you harness your anger in the right direction.

POINTS TO REMEMBER

1. Meditate. Meditation helps you keep your mind calm and stable in adversity and prosperity.
2. Read spiritual books. When we develop the habit of reading spiritual books, we also develop inner spiritual strength.
3. Change your friend circle if it has a negative impact on you.

15

PREPARING FOR THE BIGGER BATTLES IN LIFE

This science (of politics, Arthashastra) brings into being and preserves spiritual good, material well-being and pleasures, and destroys spiritual evil, material loss and hatred.

—*Kautilya's Arthashastra* 15.1.72

Friends, we are now at the last chapter of the book. Throughout this book, we have focussed on emerging a winner in various scenarios in life. Now let us look at winning in the game called life. Chanakya has a strategy for this as well. It's called grand strategy. In *Kautilya's Arthashastra*, it is called Mandala Yoni or the 'Mandala theory' (the circle of kings). It is a strategy that is used in international policymaking, international relations and diplomacy. It is also called game theory, which is the biggest strategy of permutations and combinations. Once you understand it, no questions will remain unanswered. You will be prepared for the bigger battles of life.

However, you also need to have a deep understanding of cosmic laws and principles to understand this theory. We will look at cosmic laws a bit later in this chapter, but here, let us understand the basics of the Mandala theory.

'Mandala' means circle. From the viewpoint of geometry, a circle is a very interesting figure/concept. Every point can be a starting point and every point can be an ending point. So, let us understand how Chanakya used this circle of kings in warfare. He wanted to create vijigishus or world conquerors with the help of this theory.

For example, you are the centre. You are the ruler of a kingdom. Now, look at your neighbouring kingdoms. Your immediate neighbour is your biggest threat. Since you and your neighbour share a common boundary, there is always a threat of infiltration. Chanakya calls your immediate neighbouring kingdoms your natural enemies.

So, what is the solution? Start expanding the circle slowly. Once the circle (mandala) gets expanded, other kingdoms start joining in. They become your allies.

Every neighbour has another neighbour on the other side. If your immediate neighbour is your natural enemy, what about your neighbour's neighbour? It becomes your natural friend or ally. How? An enemy's enemy is a friend.

Now, keep expanding the circle and let new kingdoms join in. And you will see many 'new' friends, enemies and allies. You will also note that some far-away kingdoms are not concerned at all with your problems. They are neutral members. But these neutral members can also be used to win the battles. This is how you make use of the grand plan or the grand strategy in politics to become a superpower. The same rules can be applied to become a vijigishu, a world conqueror.

The Chanakya Story

One day, Chanakya sat reflecting upon his own life. He had defeated Alexander the Great. The affairs of the kingdom were more or less settled. He had managed to accomplish most of what he had set out to achieve. He had been through plenty of ups and downs in his life. However, when he started to count his blessings, he realized that he had had a wonderful life, a life only few could imagine. He felt grateful for all that he had been blessed with.

He was a winner in the true sense of the term. He was a very educated scholar. He was mightier than the king himself. He had name, fame and glory. Looking back at these achievements, Chanakya took a deep breath and felt completely satisfied. He was content and desired nothing else. He no longer felt the need to achieve anything. He simply wanted to be. The mission of his life was accomplished.

As Chanakya sat deeply immersed in his thoughts, one of his students came up to him and said, 'Acharya, you have a visitor. He says he is a close friend. May I send him in?'

Chanakya peeped through the window and saw his childhood friend standing at the door. He immediately got up and ran out to receive his close friend.

'Dear friend, I am delighted to see you! You do not need permission to enter my room. Please come in.'

'I am very fortunate to have you as my friend. It is my privilege to be in the company of a great mind and a learned scholar like you. I know for a fact that many people would give their right arm to schedule an appointment with someone like you. It is truly an honour. I hope I am not interrupting...'

'Now come inside,' Chanakya said, smiling. 'There is

much to talk about other than me.'

As they settled down, his friend could not resist the temptation of appreciating Chanakya again. 'Vishnugupta, do you realize that you have actually become a Yuga-Purush?' ('Yuga' means 'an era' and 'Purush' means 'a great man'. Therefore, a Yuga-Purush is the one who has actually created an era by himself.)

His friend continued, 'What you have done for the country and humanity in general is phenomenal. Very few people have been able to do that. You have demonstrated how by sheer willpower and determination a man can achieve anything. Kings bow down before you. Your intelligence is revered everywhere. Your strategies will be remembered for ages. They will be discussed in the courts of kings. They will guide generations to come.'

'I have just one thing left to do before I complete my job on earth, my friend.'

'What is that unfinished job?' his friend asked, surprised.

'To write my version of Arthashastra...*Kautilya's Arthashastra*. Yes, you are right, I have achieved everything I set out to in this life. This body will perish, but the knowledge that I have acquired will live on through generations. I want to immortalize my knowledge and strategies through my writings. Then my job here is done.'

'That is a noble thought, Chanakya. You should write your version of Arthashastra. That will be your greatest gift to others. Your experience and wisdom need to be passed on from generation to generation. Brilliant thought indeed! I totally appreciate and support your idea.'

Then, Chanakya said something very important. 'There is one more reason behind this thought. I have seen that Chandragupta has become totally dependent on me. I am willing to guide him now, but I will not be here forever. At one point, a student has to complete his education and the guidance given by the teacher should make him free, not dependent.

'So, the best way to make Chandragupta independent is by distancing myself from him. He has to learn to be on his own, to take his own decisions. And when I am finally gone, if at all he requires my guidance, he can refer to my writings.'

This is how the idea of writing *Arthashastra* germinated in Chanakya's mind.

Chanakya Neeti

Chanakya contributed immensely to society and policymaking through his magnum opus, *Arthashastra*. Chanakya mentioned 14 Arthashastras in his own writings. It is a well-researched book. But the key question is: what is the benefit of reading *Arthashastra*?

To this, Chanakya himself answers:

This science (of politics, Arthashastra) brings into being and preserves spiritual good, material well-being and pleasures, and destroys spiritual evil, material loss and hatred.

—Kautilya's Arthashastra, 15.1.72

Arthashastra ('Artha' meaning 'wealth' and 'Shastra' meaning 'scripture') is essentially meant for those who are in the field of politics. It is a treatise on statecraft, economic policy and military strategy. However, we should not assume that *Arthashastra* is only meant for politicians and those who are part of the government systems. We will have to deal with some or the other form of politics every day of our life. So, if you want to be smart in dealing with others, this book is meant for you.

Also when we say politics, it also includes leadership. So, the book is a must-read for leaders as well. And each of us, irrespective of what we are doing, or even if we are not politicians, should think like a leader. Leadership is about responsibilities. Each of us should aspire to be a leader— it could be at our workplace, class, home or society.

Leadership does not differentiate between gender, nationality or age. Your life will change if you start thinking like Chanakya. He was a strategist and we too should start thinking like him.

Another important point is that political science as a field of study includes economics, philosophy, administration, military strategy, warfare, law and order, justice, international policy, finances, accounting systems and various other areas. In fact, *Kautilya's Arthashastra* covers over 180 topics.

Many people are of the view that spiritual people are a failure or that those who want to be successful cannot be spiritual. Both are misconceptions. People who have renounced worldly possessions cannot be considered a failure. It is a conscious decision that they have taken in search of something more meaningful, something more divine. Again, even in the midst of having a busy life, we can seek spirituality. We might have a very successful job and yet practise spirituality. We should not have a myopic vision.

By reading *Arthashastra*, we can benefit spiritually and also become successful. Like they say, '*Dono haath mein ladoo* (to have both hands full with sweets)'.

Arthashastra starts with the concept of philosophy (Aanvikshiki), control of senses (Indriya-Jaya) and Raja-Rishi (philosopher-king). *Arthashastra* also talks about merits (punya) and demerits (paap) in our lives.

The study of *Arthashastr*a also makes us financially smart. We will be able to make better financial decisions.

And then Chanakya also points out that hatred towards others is removed within you. The worst quality that we can have is hatred towards someone else. It takes away all our energies. When we hate someone, we become negative. Our mind only thinks about destruction, anger and jealously. All the creative part of our mind is lost. So, when we remove hatred from our minds and include love instead, our life changes forever.

There was a man who lived for over a hundred years. He was fit, fine and healthy. When asked what the secret of his long life was, his answer was, 'I have never allowed hatred to enter my mind. I have never hated anyone at all. I am at peace with myself and with everyone else.'

Swami Chinmayananda, the spiritual guru, too said, 'To love and be loved is the greatest achievement of life.'

Chanakya's Practical Tips

What Chanakya Says

Many of us do not have a plan for our life. We simply let things happen. Most of us have not really given much thought to the purpose of our life. We just go with the flow, which is okay sometimes, but we cannot lead a directionless life.

1. We should sit down and make a life plan. It is important that we have our goals set. We should chart out our aims and objectives. Initially, we might lack clarity and be confused. That is natural. But not making a life plan is dangerous. So, even if you stumble in the initial part, start by making a rough outline of your life. Later on, you can refine the plan with the health of experts and elders, and with experience you will anyway grow wiser.

   When you sketch out your life plan, make sure you take your responsibilities into account. So, as a student, your biggest responsibility is to study and gather knowledge. Once you are married, your most important responsibility is to take care of the family, earn money and make sure your children are educated and settled. Once your children are settled and independent, you can retire. You can spend time with your grandchildren or rekindle old friendships. You can also enjoy doing things that you have always wanted to but never really had the time, say, reading, writing, going on long walks, knitting, etc. During this stage of your life, you can also focus on your spiritual growth. Meditate, chant, do light exercises and yoga and listen to soulful music.

   You can thus have a broad plan of life. Then later you can micro-plan every little detail. However, do enjoy the twists and turns and new opportunities life gives you. Don't be rigid.

2. Set a financial plan. One of the first steps to financial success is to create a budget. When you learn the skill of creating budgets, we understand what income and expenses are. And it is important to focus on

the income part and manage the expense part. In business terms, income is also called cash flow. That is what successful businessmen and governments do—manage their cashflows.

Next, start saving and investing for the future. Your future should be secured financially. Finally, plan to give back to society. You should be generous. Plan your donations and charitable activities.

3. To be a winner in life, keep learning. Learning has no age. Learning should not end the day we pass out of school or college, or land a job. Make it a life-long process. Attend seminars and conferences. If possible try and enrol yourself for some university course. Talk to experts. Read; the importance of cultivating reading as a habit cannot be overemphasized.

   Yes, whatever be your profession, you should stay relevant. That is a must. It is called developing your professional competency. The more informed you are, the better you will perform in your field. Being knowledgeable is also a great confidence booster. Others will look up to us. When the opportunity comes teach others as well. There is no greater joy than sharing your knowledge and experiences with others.

4. It is said that the world is a cosmos, not a chaos. The world moves in a perfect order. Planets move in the right speed, the sun rises and sets perfectly every day. Nature 'knows' the seasons. All these go on perfectly without any interference from human beings.

   We should therefore respect natural and cosmic laws. There is a law of karma that governs this world.

Your actions have their own reactions. It is said that a cow finds its own calf in the midst of a herd of hundreds. That is how the law of karma works. Therefore, respect the laws and principles of nature. Keep doing your duty and success will follow. What is important is to make a start!

Swami Tejomayananda used to say, 'God knows when to give you the results of the efforts you have put. When he gives them to you later, it is good. When he gives them to you last, it is always the best.'

POINTS TO REMEMBER

1. Make a life plan. It will help you stay focussed.
2. Make a financial plan. Financial planning gives you an advantage to handle the struggles of life.
3. Keep learning. When you keep learning, you keep growing.
4. Understand cosmic laws.

CONCLUSION

Chanakya has always been my role model. It has been centuries since he wrote *Arthashastra* and *Chanakya Neeti* and yet his works are still relevant and widely referred by people.

Thank you for reading this book. I am hopeful that you will find the lessons in this book valuable and useful. Now that you have come to the end of the book, the real challenge starts. And that is applying in life whatever you have learnt so far.

To be a winner, you have to start incorporating these lessons in your life. To start with, you can choose an idea. Then gradually you can move on to other ideas. Slowly and steadily Chanakya's wisdom will start unravelling itself. Once you find its benefits, do not keep it to yourself. Share it with others as well. Knowledge is all about sharing. The more you teach, the more you learn. Besides, we have already seen in the book, winners create more winners. Readers, all the best for your battles in life. Happy winning!